THE GRASS IS ALWAYS GREENER
One Football Fan's Improbable Quest to Attend 500 NFL Games

By Brian Gushue

The Grass is Always Greener

One Football Fan's Improbable Quest to Attend 500 NFL Games

Cover Design & Interior Layout: Nicole Wurtele

All photos courtesy of Brian Gushue unless otherwise noted.

To David,

The coolest Dodgers fan I know!

Best wishes,

Brian

Published by CG Sports Publishing

CG SPORTS PUBLISHING

A Division of The CG Sports Company
Cejih Yung, CEO and Founder
www.cgsportsco.com

ISBN: 978-1-7359193-5-5

Quantity order requests can be emailed to:
Publishing@cgsportsmanagement.com

Printed in The United States of America

Former North County Times colleagues Michael Donnelly and Cathy Hendrie and Cathy's partner, Jon Norton, presented me with a special cake in a parking lot outside Lambeau Field a few hours before Game 500.

PRAISE FOR BRIAN'S BIG FEAT AND THE GRASS IS ALWAYS GREENER

- -

According to Wikipedia, the Pro Football Hall of Fame "enshrines exceptional figures in the sport of pro football, including players, coaches, franchise owners, and front-office personnel." But the hall, aside from a recent sponsor-backed initiative, has neglected a crucial category: fans. And a good case can be made that the first official inductee, accorded all the honors others enshrined get, including a gold jacket, should be the most exceptional fan of all: Brian Gushue.

The man set for himself a goal that was clearly impossible … until he went out and did it. Attend 500 NFL games, in nearly every stadium in the country? While overcoming — or rather, blasting past — physical limitations? Yup. Believe it.

But his book isn't a detailing of the nuts and bolts of his accomplishment (which I somehow still think of as impossible). It's about his love of the stadiums, the crowds, the players, the games … the GAME. Read all about. Then, someday, be sure not to miss the Gushue alcove in the Pro Football Hall of Fame.

— Arthur Salm, former book review editor of The San Diego Union-Tribune and author of the middle-grade novel "Anyway" (Simon &Schuster, 2012)*

Kudos to Brian for chasing his dream of watching his favorite sport, in person, all over the country. His passion for the NFL comes through as he shares his stories of attending more than 500 games. He also stirs up my own memories of games I have seen in person and watched on TV.

— Troy Hirsch, Sports Director, FOX 5 News San Diego

This book is dedicated with love to my parents, William Gushue Jr. and Janet Gerraty Gushue. From the time I was born it was their determination that even though I had cerebral palsy, I was to be as independent as possible in life. Every day I reap the dividends of that decision. Thanks, Mom and Dad! My love for both of you grows infinitely more with each passing day.

In addition to my parents, I extend my heartfelt thanks to my siblings, Pat, Christine, Kevin and Kitty, all of whom helped light my passion for football by giving me the chance to play my favorite sport with them and other kids we grew up with in our neighborhood.

I offer a special note of appreciation as well to Pro Football Hall of Fame quarterback Bob Griese, who was my idol as a youngster. He inspired me to always do my best when playing the game I love.

I also wish to thank other relatives of mine and so many wonderful friends who helped support my pursuit of attending 500 NFL games. Without the backing of friends and family, especially from my mother, Janet, who championed this quest more than anyone else, this book could not have been written.

Jay Paris with Brian Gushue before Game 509, the Falcons-Rams playoff game in January 2018.

FOREWORD

Any good book takes you on a journey to places that transport you far away with a compelling look into another world.

When opening "The Grass Is Always Greener: One Football Fan's Improbable Quest to Attend 500 NFL Games" it's clear that this is a deep dive into a dreamer's dream.

Brian Gushue's lofty goal was to attend 500 National Football League games.

That Herculean task had Gushue traipsing across the nation like a football nomad. From stadiums Gushue was familiar with to those he fell for at first sight, this book deftly notes the joys and challenges that earned him the distinction of being among the world's most ardent NFL fans.

That Gushue produced such a written gem is as shocking as Tom Brady winning another Super Bowl.

I crossed paths with Gushue decades ago when I was covering the San Diego Chargers for the *North County Times*. Gushue was not only a copy editor there, he was *the* copy editor.

Gushue was an All-Pro in his craft. If there's a Copy Editors Hall of Fame for those knowing the proper pronouns, punctuation and correct usage of all things scribbled, Gushue would be a first-ballot inductee.

If a journalist, like me, was fortunate enough to have Gushue review their work, two things invariably happened: Gushue would make the article sing better than when he received it, and the writer would receive a call from Gushue.

He would want to double-check passages and paragraphs, aiming for clarity and cohesiveness. Gushue wanted words to be easier to comprehend for the most important element of the writer's work — the reader.

Gushue has done that in his first book. He succinctly puts the readers in seats around NFL venues, with a first-person account of not only the game, but the significance of it, the players and what they accomplished.

Here you ride with Gushue as he crisscrosses the nation in chasing No. 500. His football weekends start on Thursday nights and by the time Sunday's games were in bed, Gushue's head hit the pillow with him closer to No. 500.

What possesses someone to push himself to achieve such a feat? Why does Gushue feel the need to always be where the action is, never mind the scratchy weather in getting there or the obstacles upon arriving?

If you're thinking that this is a football book, you're spot-on.

But this is less about X's and O's and more about a regular Joe — Gushue. He proves that when someone aspires to do something special, nothing can derail that goal.

Gushue, whose physical limitations make his endeavor even more impressive, was told countless times he'd bitten off more than he could chew. In turn, Gushue would smile that smile that seldom exits his face and spit out his upcoming schedule for the season.

It would rival the intricacies of a trucker's log, considering the time zones covered and the tight windows that Gushue's contests required.

Once, while attending a Dolphins-Chargers game, Gushue's reach across the NFL landscape was inescapable.

As a kid quarterback, Gushue was always Bob Griese of the Miami Dolphins, and that connection never wavered. When Griese was inducted into the Pro Football Hall of Fame in 1990, our future candidate for the Copy Editors Hall of Fame, Gushue, watched in awe.

So it was predictably perfect at that Dolphins-Chargers game in 2015 that a special guest interrupted Gushue at my tailgate party. Just before biting into a football-shaped doughnut, Gushue called an audible.

Would it really be right to greet Griese with a mouthful of pastry?

Gushue lowered his treat, after being tricked by others who arranged for Griese's visit.

A cool story? You bet, and it's just among the baker's dozens that fill these pages.

Griese, the quarterback of the NFL's only team to produce an unblemished record, was stunned when he heard about Gushue's march to No. 500. The admiration and respect which flowed from Griese to Gushue rivaled how Gushue felt about Griese.

They shared a love of the NFL which made them both iconic in their own rights, with digits that separated them from others.

For Griese, it's 17-0.

For Gushue, it's 500.

For those clutching this book, it adds up to a dynamite read about Gushue's affection for football, and so much more.

- Jay Paris

CHAPTER ONE
GETTING STARTED

I've been asked countless times over the years why I'm such a fan of the game of football. Very simply, as a child with a mild case of cerebral palsy, it was the one game I could play with other kids while growing up. I've watched NFL football as long as I can remember, featuring great athletes playing the game at the highest level of competition. To see that action in person as many times as I have, 550 games as of this writing, is as good as it gets for me as a sports fan.

The boost being able to play this game gave to my self-esteem when I was young was immeasurable. When one grows up with a disability, particularly a plainly visible one such as cerebral palsy, anytime you can do something of significance just as well as nondisabled youths, you feel, or at least I did, an enormous sense of pride.

And not only did I get to play, I was entrusted with the most important position on the field, quarterback, sometimes for both teams. Granted, I didn't have to face a pass rush like most QBs do. But I still had to make long and accurate throws, which I was able to do consistently, in part thanks to my God-given ability to always throw a spiral.

In addition to playing on neighborhood gridirons with my siblings Pat, Christine, Kevin and Kitty, I also had many wonderful neighbors who often took part in these games or just cheered me and others on from the sidelines. I often think about these fun times when I'm watching an exciting NFL game in person.

My lifelong thanks to Adrian and Ralph Battle, Jenny and Kevin Carter, Al Fleury, Rob Mahoney, Steve Martin, Laura and Nadine Miller, Doug, Kari and Sally Petrie, Jim Rose, Scott Roloff, Kurt Rowland, Chris, Cathy, Beth and Lee Ann Taylor, Julie True and Bob, Debbie and Wendy Wozniak for their friendship and support whenever I needed it while growing up.

Sadly, one of them, Nadine Miller, among the first of the neighborhood youths to befriend me, died at just 47 years old in 2010. Nadine and I were kindred spirits, as we both battled significant health challenges, me with cerebral palsy and her with juvenile diabetes. Whenever she saw me play sports in the neighborhood, she would always root for me to be successful. Her passing was quite sudden but thankfully painless, as her heart just stopped and she serenely transitioned to the next phase of life.

Rest in peace, Nadine, my treasured friend.

As I got older, soon after high school, I lost the ability to walk without some assistance from crutches. But I still treasure the long afternoons I spent on the neighborhood gridirons, both grass and asphalt ones, pretending I was my idol, Miami Dolphins quarterback Bob Griese. I can still hear the call in my mind, I said it to myself so often: "Griese back to pass ... throws ... touchdown Dolphins!"

As a kid I read every biography I could find on Griese. I drew inspiration from his story. He lost his father at a young age to a heart attack yet didn't let his grief keep him from becoming the star athlete his dad predicted he'd be.

While most boys acquire their love of sports from their dad, I did so from my mom. My dad's interest in the NFL ended the day Roger Staubach, who like my father graduated from the U.S. Naval Academy, announced his retirement from the game in 1980.

Interestingly, my adoption of Griese as my sports idol is inextricably linked to Staubach. More on that later.

My mom, meanwhile, was a sports fan through and through. She grew up in Lakewood, Ohio, just outside of Cleveland, cheering on the Browns, Indians and the minor league Barons hockey team. She held on to these attachments but gradually also forged new bonds with San Diego-based franchises once the Navy relocated my family there in 1969.

Eventually, my family started going to Padres games in the mid-1970s, thanks to Ray Kroc, who not only bought the team in 1974 and kept it in town but also created the 7-Up Jr. Padres Club, which enabled families to go to the ballpark several times a year at a significant discount. It's because of that program that my four siblings and I got to see Hank Aaron, Willie McCovey, Tom Seaver and other future baseball Hall of Famers in the twilight of their careers.

I can't say exactly why it was still three more years afterward that my mom took me and my two brothers to our first NFL game on Dec. 4, 1977, other than my mom felt much more comfortable at a baseball game, where fans are generally more mellow, though just as passionate in their own way. She disliked the noisy atmosphere that some fans create at football games, especially professional ones. I don't particularly mind it as long as fans are respectful to each other, regardless of their rooting interest. I've often said that a big-time football game, be it college or professional, is the sports equivalent of a stadium rock concert.

There was no mystery to why my first NFL game involved the Cleveland Browns and the San Diego Chargers. It was a matchup of my mom's old and new favorite NFL teams. I regret that other than remembering that I attended the game, I have no personal recollections from it. I'm certain, though, that I had wished my namesake quarterback with the Browns, future NFL MVP Brian Sipe, had played in the game. Sipe was a favorite of mine in part because of his local roots. He went to San Diego State University and played QB for the Aztecs. Alas, he was out that day with an injury.

I still saw something special that day when it came to Cleveland's starting signal-caller, though I didn't recognize it at the time. Filling in for Sipe was David Mays from Texas Southern University, the first black quarterback in Browns history. Two weeks earlier he had become only the fifth African American to start an NFL game at that position in the Super Bowl era. He had a pretty respectable game, too, completing 19 of 30 passes for 228 yards and one touchdown.

Unfortunately for him and Cleveland, Dan Fouts was just starting to become the Hall-of-Fame-caliber QB he's recognized as today, completing 14 of 20 passes for 237 yards and three TDs, for a nearly flawless passer rating of 149.3.

Ten months later I saw Fouts duel a fellow future Hall of Fame quarterback. My memories of that game are etched in my brain permanently.

CHAPTER TWO
LOVE THAT BOB

As near as I can recall, I chose Bob Griese as my football idol not only because of his prowess as a QB, but also because he was a worthy rival to both my older brother's and my parents' favorite signal-caller, Roger Staubach of the Dallas Cowboys. Before that, he won the Heisman Trophy while playing for the Naval Academy, often in front of my parents. Two days after my dad graduated from the academy in June 1963, he married my mom in the large chapel on campus.

While I certainly appreciated Staubach's success as a top-notch quarterback, I wanted a sports idol I could call my own. Griese seemed the perfect choice in my eyes. He not only wore the same number as Staubach, No. 12, he also was a consistent All-Pro at the position.

My memories of Griese and the Dolphins start with 1972, the year they went 14-0 in the regular season and then achieved perfection and immortality with their victory in Super Bowl VII in January 1973. As storied as that squad is, with an accomplishment that has yet to be equaled, I've always thought the 1973 Dolphins, who lost twice, were actually a better team, outscoring their postseason foes 85-33 en route to winning Super Bowl VIII.

This may be in part because I remember that season better, especially the 14-7 win over Dallas on Thanksgiving Day, payback for the 24-3 drubbing Dallas gave Miami in Super Bowl VI, one game for which I'm grateful I can't recall seeing.

That Turkey Day game was an unforgettable one for me because I saw it while in a hospital. I had fallen ill the night before and was taken there. I can't say that game cured me of whatever ailment I had but it was a wonderful tonic just the same.

Luckily, Super Bowl VIII is the first one I remember watching from beginning to end. Griese didn't pass the ball much, throwing it only seven times, completing all but one of them as the Dolphins won, 24-7. Miami's running game and defense were so dominant that day against the Minnesota Vikings he really didn't need to do so.

It bothers me today, though, when I see people interpret Griese's low passing numbers as a sign that he had little to do with Miami's success in the early 1970s. While it's true that the Dolphins' offense relied heavily on their ground game to dominate opposing defenses, what many 21st-century armchair quarterbacks don't realize is it was Griese, not head coach Don Shula or an offensive coordinator, who decided when to hand the ball off to Larry Csonka, Jim Kiick or Mercury Morris, or catch the defense off-balance with a clutch pass to Paul Warfield or Jim Mandich.

It was that kind of signal-calling that earned Griese his proper nickname: the thinking man's quarterback.

The first round of the 1974 NFL postseason brought me the greatest heartache I've ever experienced in professional sports, when Griese and the Dolphins were thwarted in their attempt to become the first team to win three straight Super Bowls. I'll have more to say on this game later.

As the 1970s progressed I continued to cheer on the Dolphins and Griese in particular. I remember feeling a greater attachment to him when I learned that, like me, he is Catholic.

For Christmas in 1977, my parents gave me a copy of *The Sporting News*, with my idol prominently featured on the cover. It celebrated another memorable Thanksgiving Day game in which he threw six touchdown passes soon after becoming the first NFL quarterback to play while wearing glasses.

When I learned that he and the Dolphins would be playing the Chargers in San Diego Stadium on Oct. 15, 1978, I made sure to let my parents know as my 13th birthday approached in August of that year that a ticket to that game would be the best gift they could give me. My mom and dad did just that, getting me a field-level seat where I had a good close-up view of the players on the field, including my favorite one, of course. It was my version of Ralphie's treasured BB gun gift in "A Christmas Story."

Looking back on that day, I can't help but notice a couple of interesting things about it. Like how the game took place on the 32nd birthday of a future idol of mine, this one musical in nature: singer-songwriter Richard Carpenter. The music he made with his sister Karen is some of the most memorable I'll ever hear. And more importantly, how lucky I was to see Griese play at all against the Chargers.

He was coming back from an injury suffered in the 1978 preseason that had sidelined him for all but a few minutes of the Dolphins first six regular-season games and didn't even start the game against the Chargers. Longtime backup Don Strock had that honor. And he led Miami to a 21-14 lead at halftime, so it would have been perfectly understandable for head coach Shula to stick with him the rest of the game. For whatever reason he didn't, and I'm forever grateful as a result. As soon as Griese took the field I started cheering my heart out for him.

And when he threw a touchdown pass to wide receiver Nat Moore for the winning score in the Dolphins' 28-21 victory over the Chargers, I was on cloud nine. That turned out to be the only time I saw Griese play in person.

After he retired from the game in 1981, I made a promise to myself that when he got the call for the Pro Football Hall of Fame in Canton, Ohio, I would be there to see him get inducted. That's where I was when he and six other greats of the game, Tom Landry, Franco Harris, Jack Ham, Ted Hendricks, Bob St. Claire and Buck Buchanan entered the hall in August 1990. I purchased his replica visitor jersey that day from the Hall of Fame gift shop.

And all three times I've been fortunate enough to attend the Super Bowl (XXXVII, XLII, XLIX), I've always made sure to wear my home Bob Griese jersey, which I had made at a Don Coryell sporting goods store in San Diego.

I thought the occasional wearing a jersey honoring Griese would be where this story ends. Turns out, I had a return ticket to cloud nine waiting for me on Dec. 20, 2015, 10 months after I had last worn his number at Super Bowl XLIX and just prior to my 458th NFL game. The Dolphins came back to San Diego that month. Griese, now a member of the Dolphins' radio broadcast crew, made the trek as well. Thanks to the efforts of San Diego-area sportswriters Jay Paris and Bryce Miller, I got to meet my sports idol face to face.

It's an old adage that one should never meet their idols because invariably you'll be disappointed in them for not living up to expectations. Well, my encounter with Bob Griese was the complete antithesis of that. He was so gracious. He let me briefly wear his Super Bowl VII ring, emblematic of the 1972 Dolphins' perfect season and he autographed the road jersey I bought at the Hall of Fame 25 years earlier. I was wearing it when he signed. It felt like he was pinning a medal on me.

I then proceeded to have a "Field of Dreams" moment with him in the parking lot of Qualcomm Stadium, playing catch, albeit with a Nerf football instead of a baseball.

Last but not least, about a month later I got a package from Griese which not only included a personally autographed football but also a signed photo from the 1972 AFC Championship Game, which featured one of the greatest performances of his career. The Dolphins and Pittsburgh Steelers were tied 7-7 at halftime. With the perfect season on the line, Shula put Griese into the game and he led them to a 21-17 win and a berth in Super Bowl VII. Without that victory, Miami wouldn't have even had a chance of completing a perfect season.

Thank you, Bob. You're a Hall of Famer off the field as well as on it.

CHAPTER THREE
WHY 500 GAMES?

I wish I could say seeing 500 NFL games was my goal from the onset, because it would have saved me considerable time and money. But it actually sprang from when I was attempting to do something similar to what many sports travel enthusiasts do, try to see a baseball game in every MLB ballpark.

I wouldn't go quite that far. I've long been a proponent of natural grass when it comes to playing surfaces for baseball and football, so I decided in the mid-1990s I would try to see a game in every MLB ballpark and NFL stadium that had a grass field.

My preference is based partly on aesthetics: I enjoy the look of grass, the feel of grass and the smell of grass. It just excites me in a way that synthetic surfaces can't. When I see those types of playing fields I can't shake the feeling I'm looking at a carpet, not a gridiron or baseball diamond.

Still, I am thankful for the vast improvement in the quality of artificial surfaces in the past 20 years. The fuzzy cement known as AstroTurf is now just a distant memory.

A curious thing happened as I started to cross venues off my lists for each sport. I found that with baseball, once I'd seen a game in a ballpark I'd never visited before, I felt no strong urge to return, whereas with football stadiums, I found that my desire to see more games increased every time I'd visit a stadium I hadn't been to yet.

It was then I realized I needed a new goal that was based on a number of NFL games, not the structures where their teams play. Sometime in the late 1990s, when I still had witnessed fewer than 100 NFL games firsthand, I chose attending 500 NFL games as my goal. I figured it was an impressive number, but not too daunting if I really applied myself.

One clarification here: as soon as I made attending 500 games my goal, I decided that only regular-season and postseason games would count toward that mark. No preseason games need apply.

Something that really helped me when it came to accruing NFL games was the very favorable work schedule I had at my place of work for most of this quest. From 1996 to 2012 I worked at the *North County Times* newspaper in northern San Diego County as a copy editor. Right from the start, my work schedule was Tuesday through Saturday, leaving open the two most important days of the week for NFL games, Sunday and Monday.

On the road to 500, I saw 70 games on Monday nights (and an additional 30 prime-time games on Thursday and Saturday nights). Without the freedom to see three or four Monday night games a year it probably would have taken me two or three more years to reach 500 NFL games. Thank you, NCT!

Late in the chase, around 2015, I added a caveat to my quest, the need to see every NFL team play in person at least 10 times, which increased my need to see games in the Midwest and back East. I'm proud that 25 percent of all the games I saw on the road to 500 were played east of Denver. So no one can say I simply West Coasted my way through this.

Now that I've explained why 500 was my goal, let's get to the fun part of reliving this football odyssey.

Instead of doing this chronologically, which could get old really fast bouncing back and forth among various stadiums, I'm going to share my experiences by venues in the order I saw my last game there on the road to 500. For example: Even though I saw my first eight games in San Diego's Mission Valley stadium, it will be the 21st venue I review. Lambeau Field in Green Bay, where I saw my milestone game, will be the 35th one.

Up first: Cleveland Municipal Stadium.

CHAPTER FOUR

A PYRRHIC VICTORY
FOR THE DOLPHINS

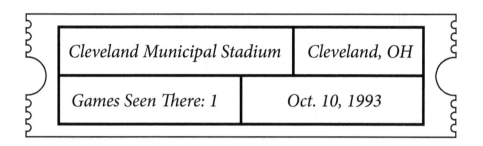

Cleveland Municipal Stadium	Cleveland, OH
Games Seen There: 1	*Oct. 10, 1993*

Unlike Sun Devil Stadium and Lambeau Field, Cleveland Municipal Stadium elicited no sense of awe for me when I saw my first and what turned out to be my only NFL game there. That's simply because I was well acquainted with the place, having already seen numerous Indians baseball games here starting in 1985, thanks to my strong family ties to the city. In fact, two weeks before the Dolphins-Browns game here, I witnessed the last win by the Indians at the stadium before they moved into Jacobs Field the following season.

That's not to say I wasn't thrilled to be here. I still remember an early autumn chill in the air that day, temperatures were in the mid-40s, the passionate Browns fans cheering and barking, yes barking, in the east end zone bleachers, where the original Dog Pound was, and taking the Rapid, Cleveland's light-rail line to and from the stadium. Actually it let people off two blocks from the stadium. Coming and going from there on crutches, they were two of the briskest walks of my life. Luckily I was still in my 20s and in pretty good shape then.

My uncle Bruce Reiman, who was celebrating his 46th birthday on this day, attended the game with me. We were sitting in seats his family had owned since the Browns started play in 1946. Among the many Browns games he attended was the first "Monday Night Football" game in 1970, when the Browns beat Joe Namath and the Jets in ABC's inaugural telecast of that long-running program.

As for the game this day, even though Bob Griese had long since retired, my allegiance to the Dolphins held firm, especially with quarterback Dan Marino leading the team. While I didn't view him with the same reverence as Griese, I still greatly admired his playing ability. On the other sideline was Browns head coach Bill Belichick. It was the first time I saw him coach a game live. This game was the only time I saw Browns QB and fan favorite Bernie Kosar play.

Miami ended up winning the game but losing its season. Marino went down late in the first half with a torn Achilles tendon. Everyone in the stands knew the injury was serious, but I didn't find out the injury was season-ending until hours later. The game itself went from bad to worse when backup QB Scott Mitchell came in and almost immediately threw a pass that was intercepted and returned 97 yards for a touchdown.

Mitchell rebounded in the second half, throwing two touchdown passes to help the Dolphins secure the win over the Browns, 24-14, but the team couldn't overcome Marino's absence and missed the playoffs that season despite a respectable 9-7 record.

Anaheim Stadium	Anaheim, CA
Games Seen There: 2	First Game: Dec. 26, 1993
	Last Game: Dec. 24, 1994

One of the few regrets I have in my quest to see 500 NFL games is that I didn't start the pursuit at least 10 years earlier, when the Rams were playing their home games in Anaheim Stadium, 2 1/2 miles from Disneyland and just a quick train ride up the coast from my home in San Diego.

One game I really wished I'd seen there took place in 1980, the Rams' first year of residency in Anaheim. Dolphins rookie quarterback David Woodley, who bridged the Griese and Marino eras, led the team to a shocking 35-14 win over Vince Ferragamo and the Rams, who were the defending NFC champions that season.

At least I can say I saw one game that way, back in 1993, when I took an express bus to Oceanside and then the Amtrak Surfliner right to the stadium. It was the Browns vs. the Rams, my second Browns game that season. This was a different squad than the one I saw 11 weeks earlier. Bernie Kosar was gone, waived and picked up by the Dallas Cowboys to back up Troy Aikman. It would be 25 years before I'd take the Amtrak Surfliner en route to another NFL game.

Playing for Cleveland that day was Heisman Trophy winner Vinny Testeverde, who had an unforgettable day, stats-wise, completing 21 of 23 passes for 216 yards and two TDs, as the Browns steamrolled the Rams 42-14. One bright spot for the Rams was rookie and future Hall of Fame running back Jerome Bettis, who I got to see play for the first time. He ran for 56 yards and one touchdown.

Fast-forward just over a year later, and I'm back at Anaheim Stadium for what would be the Rams' last home game in Orange County. They moved to St. Louis before the 1995 season. This time they were facing Washington, led by future Congressman Heath Shuler.

What I remember most about this game is that me and my friend Chuck Batte, who had driven us up there from San Diego, were among just 25,705 people in attendance. And even though I was technically there, I have to admit that for much of the game my focus was on another game taking place about 30 miles to the north at the L.A. Memorial Coliseum, where the Chiefs and Raiders were battling it out.

A Chiefs win would keep the Raiders out of the playoffs, which was my earnest hope, because I was hoping the Raiders would give up on L.A. and return to Oakland where I felt, and still do feel, they belong. The Chiefs did win and the Raiders returned to Oakland before the 1995 season. Sadly, they would leave Oakland again, this time for Las Vegas.

What a sight I must have been, seemingly watching one game, while listening to the radio broadcast of another game and cheering on action from that one. The crowd was so sparse, though, that maybe nobody noticed. The Rams also lost that day, much to my disappointment. I was hoping they'd at least end their stay in Orange County with a win.

I really enjoyed my two visits to Anaheim Stadium for NFL football, but, like trips to Disneyland, the fun ended much too quickly.

CHAPTER SIX
NOTHING COULD BE COLDER, ER, FINER, THAN AN NFL GAME IN SOUTH CAROLINA

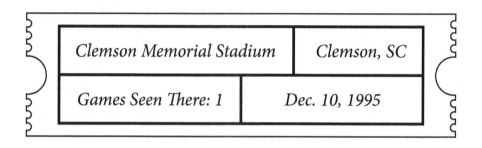

Clemson Memorial Stadium	Clemson, SC
Games Seen There: 1	*Dec. 10, 1995*

If anyone wants to know how devoted I am to seeing NFL games on natural-grass surfaces, consider this game Exhibit A.

In December 1995, I was staying in Woodstock, Georgia, just outside Atlanta, with my longtime neighborhood friend Kurt Rowland at his sister's and brother-in-law's house. We were staying there because we had plans to see an NFL game in the region. No, not in the comfortable, climate-controlled Georgia Dome, where the Falcons would be hosting their archrivals, the New Orleans Saints.

Instead, we drove two hours to Clemson, South Carolina, to see the expansion Carolina Panthers take on Steve Young, Jerry Rice and the San Francisco 49ers. According to ProFootballReference.com, the temperature at kickoff that day at Clemson Memorial Stadium was a brisk 33 degrees. The wind chill was 24.

As a resident of California, I was surprised Death Valley (the nickname for the Clemson Tigers' stadium) could be so cold.

The chill was worth it, though. This game was the first time I saw future Hall of Famers Young and Rice play in person. They lived up to their billing, as Young threw two TD passes and ran for another score, while Rice caught six passes for 121 yards. Rice was upstaged, though, by running back Derek Loville, who caught seven passes, one for a touchdown, and ran for another score.

While I was glad to get out of the cold as soon as possible after the game, I felt really good about having stayed true to my principles about natural grass and football games. Kurt and I wasted little time getting someplace warmer. The next night we were in Miami for the Chiefs and Dolphins on "Monday Night Football." It was 30 degrees warmer at kickoff.

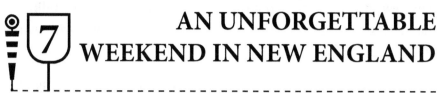

CHAPTER SEVEN
AN UNFORGETTABLE
WEEKEND IN NEW ENGLAND

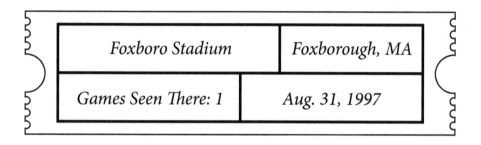

Foxboro Stadium	Foxborough, MA
Games Seen There: 1	Aug. 31, 1997

For many of my early road trips to games in the Midwest and the Eastern Time Zone, I bought tour packages. These included game tickets, lodging at five-star hotels, sightseeing opportunities and transportation. I stopped doing this when I found that I could make my own arrangements at a much cheaper cost, because I wasn't looking to do anything besides get into town, stay at a Holiday Inn Express or similar hotel, see the game and head back home. That said, I'm glad I paid top dollar for this trip because it was an unforgettable sports weekend.

We got to Boston on Friday night. The next day, our tour guides had it all set up for us to do the historical Walking Tour of Boston. I said thanks, but no. I'm going to Fenway Park to watch the Red Sox. This was back when I was trying to visit all the MLB parks with grass fields. Thanks to the location of my hotel, I was just a hop, skip and jump from Boston's subway system, which I didn't even know existed.

Before I knew it, I was only a five-minute walk from Fenway. And what a day I picked to go there. Not only was the game played in beautiful summer weather, but I also got to see the Atlanta Braves take part in their first series in Boston since leaving the city for Milwaukee nearly 45 years earlier. Both they and the Red Sox marked the occasion by wearing old-style uniforms that day. The Braves may now be visitors in Boston, but they looked right at home, pounding the Red Sox 15-2. Fred McGriff led the way for the Braves, with two home runs and five RBI.

After the game, I returned to my hotel. I was resting and trying to get to sleep when news broke about Princess Diana being involved in a car crash. Soon afterward came the sad news that the princess had died of her injuries. I'll never forget where I was when I heard those reports.

The next day was the Chargers-Patriots game. The game was Pete Carroll's regular-season debut as Patriots coach. He got off to a rousing start, as New England pummeled the Chargers 41-7. I remember being thrilled when the Chargers finally scored a touchdown on a 44-yard pass from quarterback Stan Humphries to tight end Freddie Jones. They were completely outplayed that day, but at least they avoided a shutout.

The placekicker for the Patriots that day? The seemingly ageless Adam Vinatieri, who played his last game in the NFL in 2019 at age 46. He was just a mere lad of 24 then, the first time I saw him play.

CHAPTER EIGHT
CHANGING OF THE GUARD
IN SOUTH FLORIDA

Houlihan's Stadium *(formerly Tampa Stadium)*	*Tampa, FL*
Games Seen There: 1	*Sept. 21, 1997*

When the Tampa Bay Buccaneers made their debut in 1976, they quickly became the laughingstock of the NFL, losing all 14 games that first season, the exact opposite of what their neighbors to the south, the Miami Dolphins, had accomplished in the regular season four years earlier.

Move ahead to 1997, and I couldn't help note the irony after this Monday night game that it was now the Buccaneers with a perfect record at 4-0 and the Dolphins at 2-2 who were looking for answers. This was the last year the Buccaneers played at the former Tampa Stadium, the venue ESPN's Chris Berman referred to as the Big Sombrero. I'm glad I got to see a game there. I only wish the Buccaneers had worn their orange Creamsicle jerseys. I love those uniforms and the helmets with Bucco Bruce on both sides.

As for the game itself, Miami QB Dan Marino put up good numbers (24 of 37 for 235 yards and two TDs) but Tampa Bay just had more firepower this night, both on offense and defense. Oft-maligned future Super Bowl-winning QB Trent Dilfer's passer rating exceeded that of perennial All-Pro Marino by nearly 30 points. Speaking of firepower, the venue the Buccaneers moved into the following year, Raymond James Stadium, came complete with its own munitions. More on that later.

This was also the year when the Buccaneers' Super Bowl XXXVII-winning team was just starting to coalesce. Mike Alstott (who scored two TDs this night), Derrick Brooks, John Lynch and other members of that title-winning squad were beginning to make names for themselves. I was lucky enough to be there when they won that Super Bowl. Coincidentally, members of the perfect 1972 Dolphins team took part in the coin toss for the game, including my idol, Bob Griese. Legendary Dolphins head coach Don Shula flipped the coin, which came up tails for the Buccaneers.

CHAPTER NINE

REMEMBRANCE

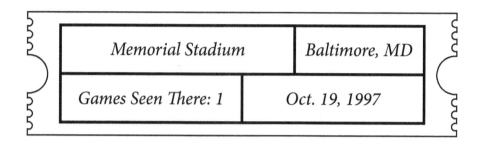

Memorial Stadium	Baltimore, MD
Games Seen There: 1	Oct. 19, 1997

When I learned the Baltimore Ravens were planning to play a couple of seasons at Memorial Stadium, I jumped at the chance to see a game there. Just looking out at the field and knowing this is where Johnny Unitas, Lenny Moore, Raymond Berry, John Mackey, Bert Jones, Lydell Mitchell and so many other legendary Colts players once displayed their football skills was awe-inspiring.

What made visiting that venerable stadium even more enjoyable was finding out it was situated in a residential neighborhood, giving it a wonderful vibe, just like Wrigley Field in Chicago.

There's not much I remember about the game itself, though I do recall hoping that Dan Marino would not only help the Dolphins win the game but throw a touchdown pass while doing so. I believed at the time that this was his first game at Memorial Stadium and I wanted him to have at least one TD pass here as he had at all the other NFL venues he had already played in. Instead, the Dolphins scored all three of their TDs that day on the ground, courtesy of running back Karim Abdul-Jabbar.

I learned much later that Marino had actually played against the Colts at Memorial Stadium in 1983, his first year in the league and the Colts' last in Baltimore. His passing stats that day? Eleven completions in 18 attempts for 157 yards and two TDs.

I also remember being very pleased that the Dolphins won this game, not just because it improved their record to 5-2 but also because they beat Ravens coach Ted Marchibroda, a fine coach who once led the Baltimore Colts. His squads always seemed to get the best of the Dolphins in crucial divisional games in the mid-1970s, nosing them out of two division titles and consequently, berths in the playoffs.

One final aspect of Memorial Stadium I do recall quite vividly is the landmark sign dedicating the stadium to U.S. service members who served in World Wars I and II. The last line read: TIME WILL NOT DIM THE GLORY OF THEIR DEEDS. That was as true when I first saw it in 1997 as it is today.

CHAPTER TEN
NINE MILES TO GRACELAND

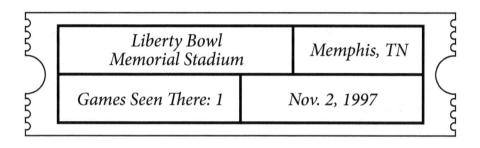

Liberty Bowl Memorial Stadium	Memphis, TN
Games Seen There: 1	Nov. 2, 1997

That's right, nine miles to Graceland from the Liberty Bowl. Of all the trips I've taken to see NFL games, this is the only time a side trip actually meant as much, if not more, to me than the game.

The game itself did have its own unique appeal. It marked the first time I saw the Jacksonville Jaguars play and the only time I ever witnessed the Tennessee Oilers compete on a gridiron. The Oilers were supposed to play in Memphis for two seasons before moving to a stadium being built for them in Nashville, but the team averaged fewer than 30,000 fans that season at the Liberty Bowl (the game against the Jaguars drew a crowd of 27,208). So team owner Bud Adams had them leave town a year early and play at Vanderbilt University in Nashville in 1998 until the stadium taking shape on the banks of the Cumberland River was ready for occupancy the following year.

With such a small crowd, I was able to get a fine seat near the 50-yard line. This was when I was still largely attending games on crutches instead of in my wheelchair. The only bad thing about that seat was that it provided no cover from the elements. It rained pretty hard a couple times during the contest, and I just had to sit there and wait those downpours out. The game itself was an entertaining one, with the Jaguars prevailing 30-24. The Oilers had a chance to tie the game and possibly take the lead late, but Steve McNair's fourth-down pass, while complete to Frank Wycheck, resulted in a two-yard loss and a turnover on downs. No Memphis Miracle for the Oilers.

Then came the highlight of my trip: Graceland. I wouldn't classify myself as a big fan of Elvis Presley, though I always respected and admired his talent when it came to music. That 20-foot wall of gold records was truly remarkable. Less so was the pea-green shag carpeting on the ceiling.

The King of Rock 'n' Roll's final resting place is a peaceful, serene setting, ideal for reflection and meditation. I don't know if I'll ever make it back to Graceland, but I'll always be thankful to the Tennessee Oilers for giving me the opportunity to go there at least once.

CHAPTER ELEVEN

NOT JUST VERY HIGH
BUT ALSO VERY COLD

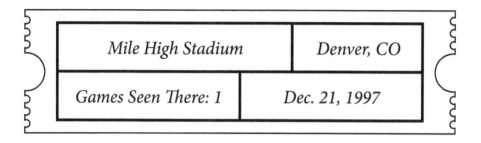

Mile High Stadium	*Denver, CO*
Games Seen There: 1	*Dec. 21, 1997*

This is the only time I've ever been OK with watching a game under an overhang. Boy was it cold that day in Denver! According to ProFootballReference.com, the temperature at kickoff was 23 degrees, with a wind chill of 16.

Since Dan Marino was still playing for the Dolphins in 1997, I was not yet a full-fledged Chargers fan. That didn't come about until he retired in 2000.

Still, as long as their games weren't against the Dolphins, I generally wanted to see my then-hometown team do well. My hopes (and my body temperature) were briefly buoyed when the Bolts took an early 3-0 lead. Unfortunately those were the only points the Chargers put on the scoreboard, as the soon-to-be Super Bowl-champion Broncos tallied the final 38 points of the contest, mostly on the right arm of John Elway, who threw four touchdown passes, the last one a 68-yarder to tight end Shannon Sharpe.

Each one triggered seismic activity in Mile High Stadium known to thrill Broncos fans and literally rattle visiting ones. I'm reminded of it whenever I attend a game at the Broncos' new home. It's similar there, but not quite the same.

Now, in the words of Bill Belichick, we're on to Cincinnati.

CHAPTER TWELVE
JASON TAYLOR HAD THE EYE OF THE DOLPHIN AGAINST THE BENGALS

Paul Brown Stadium	*Cincinnati, OH*
Games Seen There: 1	*Oct. 1, 2000*

I was so excited when I learned in the late 1990s that the Cincinnati Bengals' new stadium was going to have a grass field. I was further elated when I heard the Reds were going to install grass in Cinergy Field, aka Riverfront Stadium, the venue they'd shared with the Bengals since 1970.

This was back when I was still trying to visit all the MLB parks and NFL stadiums with grass fields. To suddenly get not one but two opportunities to do so in Cincinnati pleased me to no end. I ventured to Paul Brown Stadium in the fall of 2000 and visited Cinergy Field in May 2001. As luck would have it, the first batter up for the Reds that day was Deion Sanders, who knows a little something about pursuing goals linked to MLB and the NFL.

I only wished I had made an effort to visit Paul Brown Stadium more than once before the team switched the surface to FieldTurf in 2004. The one game I did see there was quite an interesting experience for me. It was my first Dolphins game since Dan Marino's retirement several months earlier, and I didn't know who to root for that day. I decided to just hope for an interesting game with some exciting plays. I ended up seeing a career-defining play by a future

Pro Football Hall of Famer, Jason Taylor.

For reasons I'll never understand, the Bengals had the ball at their own 36-yard line with eight seconds left in the first half and insisted on trying to pass the ball instead of simply running out the clock. Taylor went wide around a lineman, knocked the ball out of quarterback Akili Smith's hand, picked it up on one bounce and raced into the end zone as the half expired. The Bengals still had the lead at halftime, 13-10, but Taylor's improbable TD clearly swung momentum Miami's way, and the Dolphins ended up winning 31-16.

If I'm only destined to see one NFL game in Cincinnati, at least I got to see one of the NFL's greatest players show why he belongs in the Hall of Fame.

CHAPTER THIRTEEN
NEW JERSEY, NEW JERSEY

Giants Stadium	East Rutherford, NJ
Games Seen There: 2	First Game: Nov. 19, 2000
	Last Game: Oct. 14, 2001

They may still have New York as part of their names but there's no denying that the Giants (since 1976) and Jets (since 1984) play their home games in New Jersey, a state as near and dear to me as Ohio. My dad and many of his relatives were born here, as were my mom's parents. Hence, the title of this chapter is meant as both a tribute to them and a reference to Frank Sinatra's salute to New York City.

If ever Bruce Springsteen, the Garden State's favorite son, wants to write an ode to his home state, I'll be glad to let him use the title.

Getting to see NFL games in Giants Stadium I found to be especially sweet. They represent so far the only times I've ever seen NFL games in a facility that had originally opened with an artificial playing surface. This window of opportunity was sadly brief, just for three NFL seasons (2000-2002), but at least I got to see both of Gotham's former teams play there once.

The games themselves were interesting, too, albeit for very different reasons. The Lions-Giants contest in 2000 wasn't much of one, as the Lions raced out to a 28-point lead before the G-Men finally got on the board in the middle of the third quarter. One Giants fan was so upset by his team's poor play that day, he kept yelling "XFL!" the soon-to-debut spring football league which lasted only one season in its first incarnation.

Another TD late in the game by the Giants made the final score a bit more respectable. My friend and fellow *North County Times* copy editor Kip Kuduk, a die-hard Giants fan who attended the team's first game here with his dad and later joined me for a Super Bowl, says he remembers this game mostly as the one where the Lions scored a touchdown because Giants cornerback Jason Sehorn had to hold up on making a tackle because his pants had started to come loose. I checked the highlights of the game and that indeed is what happened on the touchdown Johnnie Morton scored in the third quarter.

Dolphins-Jets 2001: Barely a month after 9/11, it was really tough flying into Newark Airport, where one of the hijacked planes had taken off that terribly sad day. I couldn't bring myself to look at the actual destruction where the World Trade Center had once stood (and I had excitedly toured during my first visit to New York City in 1985).

I met my friend Jennifer MacNeil Danenberg, another former NCT colleague, at the Port Authority in New York on the eve of my one Jets game here. Lunch with Jennifer eased the anxiety I felt, and I certainly hope I helped do the same for her. She was in the vicinity when the attacks on the World Trade Center occurred.

To paraphrase Charles Dickens, this AFC East divisional game was "A Tale of Two Halves." The Dolphins got 17 points in the first half, and the Jets 21 in the second half to win. Miami had a chance to take the lead late in the game, but an interception in the end zone thwarted that opportunity. Another INT on Miami's last drive sealed the game for the Jets.

I have to give a shout-out here to my youngest sister, Kitty, who was living in New Jersey at this time. While not a fan of football (she prefers soccer), she was kind enough to provide transportation to these games and join me for both of them. Thanks, Kitty!

CHAPTER FOURTEEN
ONE IF BY LAND

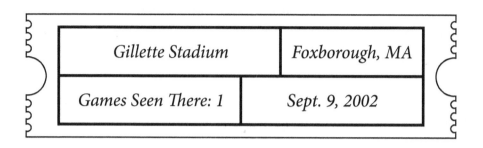

Gillette Stadium	Foxborough, MA
Games Seen There: 1	Sept. 9, 2002

If I'm destined to see only one game at Gillette Stadium (I'm still hoping the powers that be will eventually put it back on a grass footing), I'm glad it was this one. It's the only time I've attended the first regular-season game at a new stadium. Before the game, I got quite a thrill, as I met then-NFL Commissioner Paul Tagliabue.

The Patriots were coming off their first Super Bowl title, an improbable win in Super Bowl XXXVI, their fans beside themselves with joy as the banner commemorating their first NFL championship was unveiled. Who could have known back then that it was only the beginning of a dynasty unrivaled in professional football history.

This was the first time I got to see Tom Brady play in person. It was for him what would be considered an average night — 294 yards passing and three touchdown passes in a 30-14 win over the Pittsburgh Steelers. I must admit I was startled at first by the musket fire after Patriots scores by people dressed in Revolutionary War attire. But it was perfectly appropriate, given how well the Patriots christened their new home.

On a side note: not only did I get a new stadium out of this trip, I also got a new state, new to me, that is. I stayed at a hotel in Providence, marking my first (and so far only) trip to Rhode Island. Special thanks to a former *North County Times* colleague, Greg Anderson, who not only helped make it possible for me to attend this historic game, he also grilled burgers for us at our own little tailgate party.

As for my pregame encounter with Paul Tagliabue, I do remember telling him that I had made plans to see 25 NFL games during the 2002 season and its accompanying Super Bowl in San Diego. He was impressed I was pursuing such a goal, which I did achieve.

CHAPTER FIFTEEN
DEATH VALLEY DAY

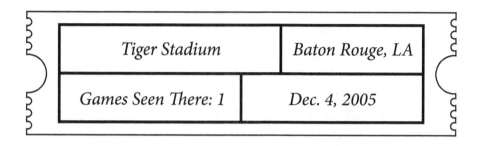

Tiger Stadium	Baton Rouge, LA
Games Seen There: 1	*Dec. 4, 2005*

This opportunity came about sadly because of the destruction caused by Hurricane Katrina, as the Saints moved their home games from the heavily damaged Superdome to the Alamodome in San Antonio and LSU's Tiger Stadium, aka Death Valley, in Baton Rouge. I reworked my schedule, passing up a Raiders-Chargers game in San Diego, to fit this game in so I would visit another stadium for NFL football and another state as well. This was the first time I'd ever been to Louisiana, outside of the airport in New Orleans. And in my opinion, you haven't really visited a state if you've never made it outside of an airport there.

This game was a reminder for me of how much I prefer upper-deck seating for sporting events. No matter how much I asked about it, LSU wouldn't or couldn't (not sure which it was) sell me an accessible seat in higher levels of the stadium, even though it was only half-full that day. I had to view it from the ground level near one of the end zones. The perspective on plays is clearer and generally easier to follow in the upper decks than at field level.

Not that there was much to see. This was one of the dullest football games I've ever witnessed, with only 13 total points scored. It's the lowest point total I've seen, matched only once seven years later by a Chargers-Browns game in Cleveland.

One player did generate some excitement: Buccaneers cornerback and likely future Hall of Famer Ronde Barber, who intercepted Saints QB Aaron Brooks three times that day. His last one came with under two minutes left to snuff out New Orleans' final chance to tie the game, as Tampa Bay prevailed 10-3.

As it turned out, I didn't have to sacrifice a Raiders-Chargers matchup to attend this game. True, I didn't see it in person, but I was able to watch it on TV, as it was the prime-time game that Sunday. The Chargers won 34-10, and my three tickets for that game ended up in very good hands. I gave them to my lifelong friend Dawn Siskowic Adams, her husband, Paul Adams, and my friend Chuck Batte.

CHAPTER SIXTEEN
HOT TIMES IN THE DESERT

Sun Devil Stadium	Tempe, AZ
Games Seen There: 22	First Game: Dec. 29, 1990
	Last Game: Dec. 24, 2005

Eagles-Cardinals 1990: My wanderlust when it comes to attending NFL games began with this one, my first game at Sun Devil Stadium and 11th overall.

This was just my second road game outside San Diego and my first outside California. As thrilled as I was, I must admit I gulped when I heard the ticket rep at the box office tell me the cheapest tickets in the upper deck were $35 apiece. I'd gotten used to paying no more than $25 for similar tickets at Chargers home games, and the one Raiders game I'd attended at the Los Angeles Memorial Coliseum in the upper deck two years earlier had set me back only $13.

Still, I happily paid the asking price. It was an overcast day that late December afternoon. According to ProFootballReference.com, the temperature at the opening kickoff was 49 degrees. I didn't mind it, though. I was having so much fun watching my favorite game being played in new (at least to me) surroundings.

I learned over the many games I saw at this place just how unforgiving the sun can be, especially if you sat on the metal bleachers without a seat cushion. You felt like an egg in a frying pan.

Randall Cunningham was the quarterback for the Eagles that day. He was just as elusive and sure-footed as he always appeared on TV.

He completed 13 of 19 passes for 172 yards and three TDs and ran for 60 yards on just four attempts. The Cardinals scored two TDs in the fourth quarter, but it wasn't enough, as the Eagles prevailed, 23-21.

Dolphins-Cardinals 1996: Dan Marino paid his only visit to Sun Devil Stadium in this contest and thankfully made it count. I saw it with my friend and former Sun Newspapers coworker Annette Kennedy. It was played in early September but had a 5 p.m. start, which thankfully pushed the mercury just below 100 degrees by kickoff. Miami raced out to a 24-0 lead at halftime en route to a 38-10 win. And much to my delight, Marino threw a TD pass in yet another NFL stadium.

Chargers-Cardinals 1998: My 10th game at Sun Devil Stadium is the only time I ever saw fans take down a goalpost. I would never condone such action but I did understand the emotion behind the fans' action. They were celebrating Arizona's 16-13 win over the Chargers, which gave the Cardinals their first playoff berth since relocating to Arizona. For me it was bittersweet, because the victory came at the expense of my then-hometown Chargers, who had mounted an impressive drive near the end of regulation to tie the game. But moments later, the Cardinals kicked a field goal, and bedlam ensued.

49ers-Cardinals 1999: This easily fits into the category of an unforgettable game. Not because of some memorable plays, but instead due to a very sad one. Future Hall of Fame QB Steve Young suffered a concussion that night that knocked him out of the game and into retirement. It's a sobering reminder of how violent the game can be and why steps should be taken to mitigate the risk as much as possible. I have some thoughts on how that can be done, which I'll divulge later in this book.

Dolphins-Chargers 2003: Speaking of my former hometown Chargers, I actually saw them play a "home" game in this stadium against Miami. The game was moved from San Diego because of major wildfires in the region. Qualcomm Stadium, where the game would have been played, was being used as an evacuation center.

Tickets for the contest were free, with distribution priority given to Chargers season-ticket holders, which included me. Sun Devil Stadium did its best to mimic a Chargers home game, with Chargers written in both end zones. Even the Chargers' touchdown cannon was brought in to lend an air of authenticity to the idea that the Chargers really were the home team.

The Bolts did something they'd never done before, wearing blue tops and blue pants for the first time in franchise history. It took a little getting used to, but it looked all right. Despite being led by Drew Brees, who was still struggling to find his way at the pro level, the Chargers were beaten handily by the Dolphins, led by ... quarterback Brian Griese.

I'd seen Bob's son play before but that was in a Broncos uniform. Seeing him suit up for the Dolphins against the Chargers, my then-favorite team, filled me with mixed emotions. It was great seeing the last name GRIESE on the field in Dolphins colors.

Ultimately, the flow of the game dictated my rooting interest, as the Dolphins romped, 26-10, thanks to Brian Griese's efficient passing. He was 20 of 29 for 192 yards and three touchdown passes. It was the only time I saw Brian Griese play for the Dolphins.

Seahawks-Cardinals 2004: My 17th game at Sun Devil Stadium represented a changing of the guard when it comes to legendary wide receivers. It was the last time I saw Jerry Rice play and the first time I saw Larry Fitzgerald in action. Rice caught one pass for 10 yards, while Fitzgerald, in his first year in the league, had four receptions for 73 yards and a touchdown, the second of his pro career.

While Sun Devil Stadium won't make my Top 10 List of venues, I'll always recall it as the site of my first three NFL games outside of California. Those relatively short trips from San Diego to Tempe, Arizona, (roughly 360 miles) no doubt paved the way for the much longer trips I would eventually take to see NFL action, starting with Cleveland in 1993.

CHAPTER SEVENTEEN
FINALLY,
A DOLPHINS HOME GAME

Hard Rock Stadium	Miami Gardens, FL
Games Seen There: 5	First Game: Dec. 11, 1995
	Last Game: Oct. 4, 2010

It took me 30 years, but I finally got to see a Miami Dolphins home game in December 1995. I'd seen my then-favorite team eight times on the road before then, where they were 4-4.

It was so much fun attending a Dolphins game where I was one of the many, not the few, cheering on Marino and Co. And Marino threw a TD pass in the game, which was nice to see. As was Terrell Buckley's knockdown of a fourth-down pass late in the game to preserve the Dolphins' 13-6 victory. It turned out to be Don Shula's last home victory as the team's head coach.

I saw two more Dolphins games here with Marino running the offense, both Dolphins victories. The first one, in September 1999, remains the only time I've ever seen the Cardinals play a game east of Arizona. It's not an intentional slight, as I actually would very much like to see them play the Bears in Chicago, their ancestral home. But for one reason or another, I've never been able to do that.

My last game there with Marino at the helm, in December 1999, turned out to be the only game I've seen where no touchdowns were scored. It was a contest of field goals, with the Dolphins prevailing 12-9 over the Chargers after John Carney's attempt to tie the game clanged off one of the uprights.

In the post-Marino era, I've had a very rainy Christmas at this venue, and a tutorial by the New England Patriots on the many ways a team can score a touchdown in football.

Also of note, Hard Rock Stadium actually used to be in Miami. But now it resides in Miami Gardens. It didn't move. The new city of Miami Gardens was incorporated in 2003, and the stadium's location was included within the new city's boundaries.

The Christmas 2006 game, the one time I've attended a game on what will always be my favorite holiday, was a soggy, losing, Monday-night affair against the Jets. It's notable not for the game itself but for then-Dolphins head coach Nick Saban saying over and over again in his postgame press conference that he had no interest in the vacant University of Alabama head-coaching job.

This game is also significant for me because it was the last of three games I attended in three days, the only time I've done this. The first two were easy: A Saturday night matchup between the Chiefs and Raiders in Oakland, then going across San Francisco Bay to see the Cardinals play the 49ers before catching a red-eye flight to Miami, with a stopover in Detroit early Christmas morning.

The last time I visited this place, October 2010, I was reminded of the overall greatness of the Patriots and the many ways the New England dynasty conquered its foes. In a 41-14 rout of Miami, the Patriots scored touchdowns via pass, run, kickoff return, blocked field goal return and interception return. Tom Brady was his usual efficient self, completing 19 of 24 passes for 153 yards and one touchdown pass. Actually a pretty ordinary night for a quarterback of his caliber. Then again, when so many of your teammates are scoring TDs on their own, a quarterback doesn't need to do much.

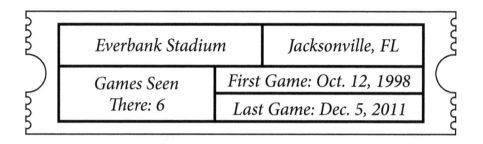

Everbank Stadium	Jacksonville, FL
Games Seen There: 6	First Game: Oct. 12, 1998
	Last Game: Dec. 5, 2011

The first two games I saw here were both intrastate affairs, with the Dolphins coming north to play the Jaguars. The first one, in October 1998, was also the beginning of the rivalry, at least outside the preseason, as it was the initial regular season contest between these Florida-based squads.

Held under the glare of what was then ABC's "Monday Night Football," it was quite a raucous atmosphere. The game was tied at 21 late in the fourth quarter until Mark Brunell connected with Kennan McCardell on a 56-yard TD pass. The Jaguars' defense then shut the Dolphins' offense down the rest of the way, prevailing 28-21.

While that game had a party atmosphere fans of both teams could enjoy, the next time the Dolphins visited their in-conference cousins in January 2000, it turned into a wake as far as Miami supporters, including myself, were concerned.

Even though because of a ticketing mix-up I only saw three quarters of this contest, it will always be the saddest game I've ever seen. By the time I got settled in my seat, it was 24-0 Jaguars. Then I blinked and it was 31-0. In what would be his final game, Dan Marino completed just 11 out of 25 passes for 95 yards, one touchdown and two interceptions, as Jacksonville steamrolled Miami 62-7.

Bob Griese will always be my favorite quarterback because of how he inspired me to play football. Dan Marino will always be second on that list because of all the heart and gallantry he displayed on the gridiron, along with his immense talent as a signal-caller. As poorly as he played that day, he never stopped fighting. That's why, even though the end result broke my heart, I'm glad I at least got to witness the final touchdown pass of his legendary career.

Near the end of the game, I was interviewed by a Miami TV station. At first, the reporter thought I had on a Marino jersey. I actually was wearing the Bob Griese road jersey I'd bought at the Pro Football Hall of Fame when he got inducted and later signed for me. I expressed my deep sadness for how things had gone that day and hoped that it wouldn't be the end of the line for him because I enjoyed watching him play so much, especially in person.

Unfortunately for me and millions of other die-hard Dolphins fans, Marino did indeed hang up his spikes a few months later.

You may not have won that elusive Super Bowl title, Dan, but you'll always have my undying admiration for how hard and well you played the game of football.

Colts-Jaguars 2008 and 2009: My next two visits here involved another legendary quarterback, Peyton Manning. In two games barely less than a year apart, the Colts prevailed over the Jaguars 31-24 and then 35-31, both times overcoming third-quarter Jacksonville leads. In the latter contest, Indianapolis' win made it just the third team to start a season 14-0, a mark which was then blemished the following week with a loss to the Jets.

Chargers-Jaguars 2011: My most recent game in northern Florida, which I witnessed with my friend and former coworker Annette Kennedy, had the Chargers winning 38-14, thanks largely to quarterback Philip Rivers' highly efficient play — 22 of 28 passing for

294 yards and three touchdowns. Not only was it a dominant win for the Bolts, it helped Annette and me complete our Chargers/Florida trifecta. With this game, we'd now seen them play the Dolphins in Miami, the Buccaneers in Tampa, and the Jaguars in Jacksonville.

Candlestick Park	San Francisco, CA
Games Seen There: 49	First Game: Nov. 23, 1997
	Last Game: Dec. 23, 2013

Appropriately, I visited this venue 49 times for NFL games. It wasn't a goal of mine; it just worked out that way. Apologies to Question Mark and the Mysterians, whose hit song "96 Tears" I reference with this chapter's title.

Tears can be for joy or sorrow, which is fitting because I was always of two minds about this place. It was without question a nightmare to get in and out of, especially if you didn't have a car. There were no hotels close to the stadium, so I would have to take a hotel shuttle to the airport, then take a BART train to the Balboa Park Station, then take a bus to the stadium. After the game was over I would have to repeat the process. This usually took about an hour and a half to two hours each way.

Once I was there, though, I was thrilled to be in a venue with so much history. Not just sports history either, as The Beatles played their last official concert here in 1966. And just before the Stick was razed a few years ago, the last event that took place there was a concert by Paul McCartney.

The Giants and especially the 49ers did produce a lot of memorable moments here. I wasn't present for The Catch or The Catch II, but I did see my share of notable games there:

Bears-49ers 2000: The first one that really stands out to me was Jerry Rice's final home game with the 49ers. It was officially Jerry Rice Day, but he got upstaged by fellow future Pro Football Hall of Fame wide receiver Terrell Owens. He caught 20 passes in that game, setting a record that stood until 2009, when Denver's Brandon Marshall pulled in 21 passes in a game against the Colts. On a personal level, the 17-0 San Francisco win was the first shutout I ever witnessed in person.

Rams-49ers 2001: Rams 30, 49ers 26. While it was an exciting game, what made this one unforgettable was the fact that it was one of the first NFL games held after the Sept. 11 attacks. It was preceded by a very moving tribute to the victims, and also contributed to the sense of normalcy so many Americans, myself included, sought in the days following the tragedy.

Steelers-49ers 2011: There was a power outage right before the game and another during the contest, which delayed the proceedings by 15 minutes. It's really something when a place that big, with nearly 70,000 people in it, suddenly goes dark and you feel like you're surrounded by fireflies as people use cellphones, lighters and glow sticks.

San Francisco won 20-3, but in the days after the game I learned there had been some talk of resuming it in Oakland the next day if the power couldn't have been restored a second time. I kind of wish that had happened, to see an NFL game start at one venue and end in another. What a unique experience that would have been!

Speaking of the Jim Harbaugh era, which began that season, that period was very exciting, particularly in three years at Candlestick: two NFC West division titles and a berth in Super Bowl XLVII. While his squads may have fallen short of the ultimate triumph, I'll forever be thankful to them for the three home playoff games they gave me in 2012 and 2013. I always considered postseason action a bonus when it came to chasing my 500 games goal. I could never count on them so I was very appreciative when those opportunities arose.

As for those playoff games, all three were memorable, with Alex Smith outdueling Drew Brees and the Saints in the 2011 NFC divisional round, followed by a heartbreaking overtime loss to the Giants in the 2011 NFC Championship Game, and then Colin Kaepernick running and passing the Packers silly for 444 total yards in the second round of the following postseason.

As much as sports fans wish otherwise, most stadiums close without anything special happening in their final game. Not Candlestick. In the final game at the venerable venue on Dec. 23, 2013, NaVorro Bowman's late-fourth-quarter, 89-yard interception return for a touchdown against Matt Ryan and the Falcons was immediately dubbed "The Pick at the Stick." It clinched the game and a playoff berth for the 49ers.

My wheelchair space could not have been better positioned to see the play. I was in the upper deck near the end zone Bowman was racing toward.

A really touching moment occurred at halftime of that farewell game. With Dwight Clark present, the 49ers spray-painted the area in the end zone where Clark made "The Catch," the legendary play that launched the 49ers' dynasty of the 1980s. Sadly, Clark passed away in 2018 from ALS.

Thank you, Candlestick Park, for giving me so many wonderful memories that made all the transportation hassles worth it.

CHAPTER TWENTY
GUESS I'LL HAVE TO SETTLE FOR A 9-GALLON HAT

NRG Stadium	Houston, TX
Games Seen There: 9	First Game: Sept. 22, 2002
	Last Game: Oct. 9, 2014

My dad had a tradition when it came to birthdays for me and my four siblings. For our 12th and 15th birthdays, we could watch any movie then playing in theaters in honor of our special day.

For my 12th birthday, I chose "The Bad News Bears in Breaking Training." I was enthralled by the scenes in the Astrodome. It really did seem to me like it could be, as it was billed, "The Eighth Wonder of the World." This was years before I had my change of heart about synthetic field surfaces.

Fast-forward 25 years later to 2002, and the Astrodome looked rather puny in the shadow of what is now known as NRG Stadium. I witnessed nine NFL games at this 21st-century architectural wonder.

A note of appreciation here for my friend Kathryn Iribarren, formerly the Texans' coordinator of disabled seating at NRG Stadium. She always helped me secure ADA tickets, making sure they were in the upper reaches of the stadium, always my preferred vantage point. Thanks, Kathryn!

Starting in 2006, I made a concerted effort to try and visit what was then called Reliant Stadium at least once a year. And not just because it was a great venue for football. It also offered the best barbecued brisket sandwich I have ever tasted. It was always the first thing on my mind once I got inside the place. It was sold at stands under Bum Phillips' name. I've yet to taste a sandwich at a sporting event equal to it.

Of the games I attended here, three were unforgettable.

Colts-Texans 2002: "The Ninth Wonder of the World." My first one here was actually my second Texans game in what was their inaugural NFL season. I saw them lose the week before, 24-3, to the Chargers in San Diego, in what was only their second regular-season game ever. It didn't get any better for the Texans against the Colts, losing by the almost identical score of 23-3. Still, I came away very impressed with this venue, the first one in the NFL with a retractable roof.

Bengals-Texans 2012: "A Texas-Sized Triumph." This playoff game was especially sweet because it was the first one in the Texans' history and it was wonderful to see the loyalty of longtime fans be rewarded with a dominating victory, 31-10, with TDs scored by defensive end J.J. Watt, wide receiver Andre Johnson and running back Arian Foster (two).

Colts-Texans 2014: "The Last Roundup?" My most recent visit, a Monday night matchup against AFC South rival Indianapolis. Joining me for this game was another fellow *North County Times* alum, Erica Warren Holloway and her husband, Robert, who now live in Houston.

This game featured two of the brightest young stars in the league at the time: Andrew Luck of the Colts and J.J. Watt of the Texans. Indianapolis jumped out to a big lead, 24-0, with Luck throwing two TD passes, but Houston slowly clawed its way back into the game. The Texans cut the Colts' lead to five points, 33-28, after Watt picked up a Luck fumble and rumbled 45 yards for a touchdown. The roar of the fans was so loud I thought they might blow the retractable roof right off the building. Unfortunately, the Texans could get no closer that night.

And that could be my last game there. I had hoped to get at least a 10th, but in the Texans' first regular-season game at NRG Stadium against the Chiefs the following season, there were problems with the grass field, as there had been in the past. So the Texans decided to go to with FieldTurf full time at the facility instead of just for the college games played there.

While I won't go back to this facility for NFL football unless a grass field is put back in place, I don't begrudge the Texans for the decision they made. As much as I champion grass fields for baseball and football, player-safety concerns must be paramount. So if a team isn't able to maintain a top-flight natural surface, then I say go with the fake stuff. I still won't attend any games where it's installed but I'll bear no ill will against teams that play their home games on it.

CHAPTER TWENTY-ONE
HALFTIME

Since I've reached the halfway point of this book, I'd like to pause here for my own personal halftime and talk about the state of pro football as it's played today, what I think can and should be done to make a more enjoyable game for fans, and more importantly, a safer one for the athletes who play it.

My first suggestion would be to reduce the time of quarters from 15 minutes to 12 minutes apiece. This is the length of quarters in high school. Why not mandate that for the college and professional levels of the game, too? If Major League Baseball can have seven-inning games, why can't pro football have 48-minute games?

There is recent precedent in shortening game time in the NFL. In 2017, the length of the overtime period was cut from a maximum of 15 minutes to no more than 10 minutes.

I also would require each team to have at least two bye weeks in a season, something that was done during the 1993 NFL season, and no longer allow teams to play Thursday after playing the previous Sunday. Thursday games would be permitted provided they took place at least seven or 10 days after a team's previous game.

I realize hard hits are part of the game, and they can't be legislated out of it. Still, if the amount of game time is reduced and recovery time increased, I think that would be better in the long term for athletes and the game itself. Besides, greatness will always find its way to the top no matter how long the seasons or games are.

Jim Brown played half his career when the NFL slate was only 12 games. Roger Staubach played nearly his entire career making no more than 14 starts per season. When their names and those of their contemporaries are discussed, what's talked about most is how well they played, not how many snaps they took or the statistics they compiled. Individual statistics aren't meaningless in football, but they aren't as revered as they are in baseball because in that sport collective effort isn't always required to achieve them.

TV contracts are constantly being revisited and extended, so I think there would be room for flexibility by the networks. Plus, I can't help but believe that networks would like a return to the days when NFL games fit neatly into three-hour programming windows and didn't wreak havoc with their prime-time lineups. I'm sure the constant spillover of NFL games creates problems for networks with their nonsports programming and related advertising. With fewer spots to fill, advertisers would likely pay higher rates.

One other change I would institute is winding the clock after an incomplete pass after the ball is ready for play, just as it is after a running play. That alone would probably shorten games by at least five minutes. I'd still allow for incomplete passes to stop the clock until the next snap of the football after the two-minute warning in the first half and with five minutes or less in the second half.

I'd also reduce the number of preseason games to no more than two per team — one home game, one away game.

Finally, I'd standardize the rule for catching passes on the sideline or boundaries of an end zone. High schools and colleges have it right: one foot is all a receiver needs to be in bounds for a catch. The NFL should make this a unanimous rule. This would make for more great catches and fewer replay challenges.

Now let's get out to Empower Field at Mile High and resume the countdown.

CHAPTER TWENTY-TWO
FAVRE & TEBOW:
MILE HIGH MAGIC

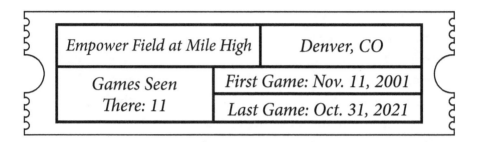

Empower Field at Mile High	Denver, CO
Games Seen There: 11	First Game: Nov. 11, 2001
	Last Game: Oct. 31, 2021

If you ever go to a game here and you're rooting for the visiting team, pray that your quarterback is especially accurate that day. Otherwise, the long, drawn-out call of "IN-COM-PLETE" after every misfire will haunt you for days if your team loses.

I've been fortunate to attend 11 games at this stadium. I've attended most with my friend Mike Goodman, who I got to know from our days at San Diego State University. We never had any classes together, but we kept striking up conversations in the hallways near the journalism classrooms.

Thanks so much for all your help getting to and from many of these games, Mike. I hope you enjoyed them as much as I did.

Two games that Mike and I attended together which stand out most for me here are the Packers-Broncos game on Oct. 29, 2007, and the Jets-Broncos game Nov. 17, 2011. Two quarterbacks of vastly different skill sets led their teams to victory on those dates.

First up: The gunslinger, Brett Favre. The Broncos drove 90 yards late in the fourth quarter to kick a field goal with three seconds left to tie the Packers at 13.

But on the first play after the overtime kickoff, Favre coolly dropped back and threw the ball 50 yards to wide receiver Greg Jennings, who took it the rest of the way for the 82-yard winning touchdown. From our vantage point, Mike and I could see just how accurate Favre's throw was and that it would win the game. What an ending!

The other QB? An enigma. You never knew what kind of performance you'd see from Tim Tebow. Luckily for Broncos fans on that night, Tebow had his magic when he led the team 95 yards for the winning score. I can still see him scrambling wide around the right end to evade the Jets' pass rush and run the football 20 yards into the end zone in the final minute. *The Denver Post* had it just right the following day with the headline "In the nick of Tim."

One final note about the Packers-Broncos game I saw here.

Anyone who's ever seen a Green Bay Packers game outside of Lambeau Field has seen firsthand how well their fans travel to away venues. I saw plenty of Packers fans at this game, too. What struck me as unique though, was how many mixed couples there were at this Monday night game — mixed in terms of rooting interest. One person would be dressed in Broncos garb and the other would be attired in Packers gear. Even so, I noticed many were holding hands as they walked into the stadium. What a touching display of love and sportsmanship.

Post-500 commentary: My first game here after reaching the 500-game mark was Lions-Broncos in 2019, but not with Mike. He and his family have moved to Northern California, where we hope a 49ers game or two is in the cards in the near future. Stepping in to help me attend more NFL games here is another SDSU colleague, Dan Wildhirt. It was not only Dan's first NFL game, it was also the first for his son, Jake, who was able to join us.

Given my preference to avoid cold-weather games post-500, I tempted fate with a game that took place three days before Christmas.

Mother Nature, though, gave me an early gift; the high that day was 67, 25 degrees above normal.

I'd be remiss if I didn't mention Dan's unique contribution to my career in journalism. In the late 1980s, shortly after we graduated SDSU, Dan had a part-time job editing a newsletter called "The Slice" for Domino's Pizza outlets and asked me to proofread it for him. It was my first professional job in journalism. My payment for services rendered? Pizza, of course! When you're in your early 20s, getting free pizza is just as enjoyable as earning a little bit of money.

CHAPTER TWENTY-THREE
A QUIET PIRATE'S LIFE FOR ME

Raymond James Stadium	Tampa, FL
Games Seen There: 9	First Game: Dec. 6, 1999
	Last Game: Nov. 3, 2016

This place really plays up the buccaneer motif, complete with a pirate ship in the seating area behind one of the end zones. It's a nice touch. I only wish it wouldn't fire so many volleys during games: six for touchdowns, three for field goals and one for every time the Buccaneers enter their opponents' red zone (at or inside the 20-yard line). That sound echoes throughout the stadium. I'm rather sensitive to sudden loud noises, so I always try to be as far away from the pirate ship as possible.

Of the games I've seen here, four stand out in my memory. The first was Sept. 23, 2002, when the Buccaneers beat the defending NFC-champion St. Louis Rams 26-14 on a Monday night. The game was a sneak peek of what I would see four months later in Super Bowl XXXVII. Mike Alstott scored a TD from two yards out, and Derrick Brooks returned an interception for a touchdown, one of four Kurt Warner passes the Buccaneers picked off, similar to what happened to Raiders QB Rich Gannon the following January.

As visiting NFL fans know, few things are sweeter in life than watching your team win a game on the road. That's how I felt when I saw the Chargers beat the Buccaneers here in 2008, 41-24. My friend Annette Kennedy and I felt so good upon leaving the game, knowing that even though we were vastly outnumbered by Buccaneers fans, our side had prevailed that day. We were careful not to gloat, though. You never know when things might go the other way, which is just what happened when the Chargers returned to Tampa four years later and lost 34-24.

The first time I saw an NFL game in Tampa was at Houlihan's Stadium in 1997, the first year the Buccaneers went with their current uniforms. Pewter Power, they call it. It's what they wore while winning Super Bowl XXXVII, but I still hoped someday to see a return of the Buccaneers' original threads, the Creamsicle jerseys and Bucco Bruce on the side of the helmets.

Turns out that was just what I got on Dec. 4, 2011, when Tampa Bay played Carolina. Not only did the Buccaneers wear the outfits I prefer, the field was marked like it was before the change in team colors.

This was the first time I ever saw Cam Newton play in person, and I realized just what an imposing presence he is. Newton, in his rookie season as the Panthers' quarterback, passed for 204 yards and ran for 54 that day in leading the Panthers to a 38-19 win. He likes to project himself as Superman. All he was missing in this game was the cape.

Another memorable game here came Nov. 3, 2016, when a fellow former Sun Newspapers colleague, Thomas Neumann, joined me for a Falcons-Buccaneers contest. I hadn't seen Thomas in 20 years. We had a wonderful time watching the game and catching up with each other. One of the nicest fringe benefits of this state-hopping hobby of mine is how it's enabled me to reconnect face to face with so many people from my past who now live far away from San Diego.

Special thanks to Buccaneers officials Michael Vanduyn and Tyler Frattura, who helped provide me access to tickets for recent games here, including the most exciting one I've ever seen at this venue, in October 2016, when the Raiders came to town for another tussle with the Buccaneers over which team would have bragging rights to raise the Jolly Roger afterward. Oakland prevailed 30-24 in overtime in a nearly four-hour game.

While I was disappointed the Buccaneers didn't win, I was happy for my friend and fellow former *North County Times* colleague, now-novelist James Curran as he rooted his Raiders on to victory. I enjoy making it possible for my friends to see their favorite NFL team play in person, especially if it's the road team.

Why? Because I love seeing fans being true to their teams, especially in hostile environments. I respect that kind of loyalty in sports, as long as one doesn't cross the line into obnoxious behavior. None of my friends has ever acted that way. If any of them did, I'd make them sit right next to the cannons on that pirate ship!

CHAPTER TWENTY-FOUR
A GAME'S NOT REALLY OVER HERE UNTIL JAMES TAYLOR SINGS

Bank of America Stadium	Charlotte, NC
Games Seen There: 6	First Game: Nov. 15, 1998
	Last Game: Dec. 11, 2016

Dan Marino did throw a touchdown pass in this stadium in his one appearance here, and my first, in 1998. It won't say so in the box score, but I know he did it because I saw the play. It was a 10-yard completion to Lamar Thomas that was wiped out by an offensive pass interference penalty by fellow wide receiver Orande Gadsden. Were it not for that infraction, Marino would have been credited with at least one TD pass at every NFL stadium in which he played.

At least the Dolphins still won the game, 13-9. If I had to choose between the two, I'd take the victory every time.

Special thanks to former *North County Times* colleague Lydia Craver, who helped secure a ticket for me for this game, the Dolphins' first visit to Charlotte.

The next time I saw the Dolphins play at BofA Stadium, in 2009, history was on my side. It was my 300th NFL game.

Again the Dolphins won, this time 24-17 behind the running of former Heisman Trophy winner Ricky Williams. He rushed for 119 yards and two touchdowns that night. What also stood out in my mind that night was I was able to get a four-pack of glazed Krispy Kreme doughnuts at the game to go with Domino's cheese pizza. Just right for a fan of simple tastes such as myself.

In my most recent game here, I completed another NFL-related quest decades in the making. When I saw the San Diego Chargers play the Panthers in December 2016, it meant I had now seen the Chargers play in every NFL stadium with a grass field at that time. I kept reminding myself of that fact so I'd forget how cold it was that day. The thermometer read 37 degrees at kickoff but I'm sure it got down around freezing afterward, particularly with the wind chill factored in.

Shivering in the stands with me that day was my friend Jaime Bowden, a former *North County Times* colleague, who is now a teacher. She said during the game that her face felt frozen!

When it comes to attending games with me, Jaime has been a real trouper. She not only endured freezing temperatures at this game, previously she weathered monsoonal conditions in Cleveland for a Chargers-Browns game in 2012, then had to drive right back to West Virginia before Superstorm Sandy made landfall. And though we didn't technically attend the game together, Jaime went with her mom to my only snow game so far, the soon-to-be discussed Chargers-Steelers contest in 2008.

As cold as it was, though, I still made sure to hang around for a Panthers postgame tradition, hearing James Taylor's "Carolina In My Mind." It's not the first tune played after the game, such as "Lights" by Journey at 49ers games, but it's still one I have to hear before vacating the premises.

Post-500 commentary: Last spring I learned the Panthers were replacing the natural-grass surface here with FieldTurf, placing BofA Stadium out of bounds as far as my future NFL games are concerned. I may not have visited this place often, but that was solely because of the great distance between San Diego and Charlotte, well over 2,000 miles. It's one of the best places to see a football game.

And if the playing surface ever reverts back to natural grass, to paraphrase another great James Taylor song: "I'll come rolling (in my wheelchair) to visit again."

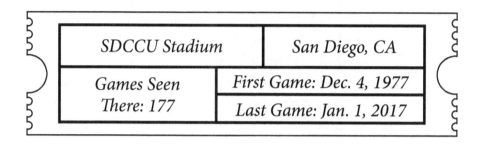

CHAPTER TWENTY-FIVE
THERE'S NO PLACE
LIKE HOME

SDCCU Stadium	San Diego, CA
Games Seen There: 177	First Game: Dec. 4, 1977
	Last Game: Jan. 1, 2017

Before I say anything about the NFL games I witnessed here, a few words about tailgating, which San Diego fans have perfected over the years. I was lucky enough to take part in not one but two first-class tailgate parties before games here.

One was run by my friend, sportswriter Jay Paris, who worked with me at the *North County Times*. The other was hosted by a friend of mine from high school, Lynn Reiter Woodhead, her husband, Jim Woodhead, and good friends David and Frances Kirsten and Pete Olah. My contribution to each gathering? Krispy Kreme doughnuts.

Tailgate parties are a fun way to start game day, especially if it's a big game. Lots of great food and camaraderie. The only thing better is watching the game itself.

The Woodheads' tailgate party not only featured delicious snacks and entrees, but also a portable TV set, great for keeping tabs on the morning NFL games.

Jay was ably assisted with his tailgate party by two wonderful couples, *Orange County Register* sportswriter Steve Fryer and his wife, Kathy, and Kipp and Ann Bennett, who always took the time to grill the kind of food preferred by carnivores, especially me.

Jay's gatherings drew not only fellow journalists, but also living legends of the game. American Football League founder and Kansas City Chiefs owner Lamar Hunt, was known to drop by occasionally. And it was at one of his tailgate parties in 2015 that I realized my lifelong dream of meeting Bob Griese.

One extraordinary athlete was even one of the regulars there: two-time tennis Grand Slam winner Rod Laver, Ann Bennett's stepfather, a man who is as nice off the court as he was ferocious on it. I'll never forget the time I invited my friend and fellow NCT alum Cathy Hendrie, a Wisconsin native, to join me for a Packers-Chargers game here in 2011. The Packers won 45-38, but Cathy's day was made before kickoff, when she got to meet Rod and have her picture taken with him.

One last note about Laver. It turns out we have a unique bond. Not only are we both die-hard football fans, we're also fellow 8-9ers, both born on Aug. 9.

A special thank you to the construction crews who expanded the stadium to 70,000 seats back in the late 1990s. Thanks to their efforts, and a new wheelchair section with five companion seats and four wheelchair spaces, I was able to invite two people to join me for each Chargers home game, making it easier to fill requests from family and friends, adding to their enjoyment and mine.

It was always a little extra special when both a family member and a friend, sometimes theirs, sometimes mine, sometimes ours, took part in the fun here. My sister Christine and her friend Cliff occasionally joined me, as did Kevin and Kitty and their friends. No such luck with Pat, who never joined me at the Murph again after that first game we saw together in 1977. It wasn't because of anything I did. He just loathed the Chargers as much as I've seen anyone ever hate a sports franchise.

Still, we have gotten in more NFL action together. Pat joined me for my first true milestone game, No. 100, in Oakland in 2000 and another game in Arizona.

Attending football games with my siblings and childhood friends, including Doug Petrie and Kurt Rowland, always brings home the memories I have of us playing the sport together, some of the happiest times of my childhood.

Having two tickets to dole out for each game also made it easier for me to invite friends who were fans of the visiting team in town that day. I really enjoyed offering them what might be the only chance to see their team play that year, especially if it was based in the Midwest or the Eastern Time Zone. One friend in particular I enjoyed inviting when his team was visiting San Diego was former NCT colleague Gig Conaughton.

A true blue fan of the Colts, Gig's history with seeing the Colts play in person in San Diego goes all the way back to 1970, when they faced off against the Chargers in the opening game of the regular season. The then-Baltimore Colts prevailed 16-14 in a contest that foreshadowed exactly how their season would end nearly five months later in Super Bowl V, with a game-winning field goal by rookie kicker Jim O'Brien. Gig's recall of events is so good I can still hear him talk about the drive Johnny Unitas led, including a clutch throw to WR Roy Jefferson, to get O'Brien in position for his successful kick.

Most of my early games at the Murph, as I affectionately still like to call it, involved the Dolphins. While my first Dolphins-Chargers game there was an unquestioned triumph, with Griese leading Miami to victory in 1978, the next six were mostly heartache for this Fins fan. I think the toughest to take was the 22-21 loss in a divisional playoff game in January 1995, followed closely by the 1984 contest, when Buford McGee scored the winning touchdown in overtime to thwart the Dolphins' bid for a second perfect season. Miami had come into the game with an unblemished 11-0 record.

I saw that destiny-denying game with my friend Randy Betts, who several years earlier fulfilled a wish of mine in a different sport when he introduced me to his friend Jim Kaat, a three-time MLB All-Star and favorite ballplayer of mine. Like my encounter with Griese in 2015, every time I met Kaat in the late 1970s and early 1980s, he could not have been more gracious. I do hope he gets the call from Cooperstown in the near future. His 283 wins and 16 Gold Gloves are a testament to his durability and consistency.

Two years later, full of optimism as the Dolphins started the regular season in 1986 in San Diego, my hopes were dashed early. Chargers running back Gary Anderson set the tone for the day, with an unforgettable vault and somersault into the end zone for the game's first score. After that, there was nothing Marino and his teammates could do to keep pace with Dan Fouts and Co., losing 50-28.

Three more losses followed, including the very painful postseason defeat in January 1995 that I was unable to attend. Thankfully, the last time I saw Marino and the Dolphins play the Chargers in San Diego in November of that year, when they were still my team, they emerged victorious, 24-14.

There are several other unforgettable games I saw here not involving the Dolphins; here are seven, plus two honorable mentions.

7. "Lionel 'Little Train' James wins it." Nov. 10, 1985: Of all the rivalry matchups I saw here, the one I witnessed the most often was Raiders-Chargers. Surprisingly, the first time I saw them play each other, on Nov. 10, 1985, remains the best one. The Chargers put together a late fourth-quarter drive, culminating in a TD pass involving two future Hall of Famers, quarterback Dan Fouts and wide receiver Charlie Joiner, to force overtime.

The real star of the game, though, was 5-foot-6 Lionel "Little Train" James, who had 345 all-purpose yards, including the winning touchdown, a 17-yard run in overtime. Final score Chargers 40 Raiders 34. NBC Sports announcer Don Criqui put it best: "The smallest man in the NFL is eight feet tall. Lionel 'Little Train' James wins it."

6. Never Leave a Game Early. Nov. 22, 1998: Chiefs vs. Chargers. When people ask me why I never leave a game early, this is my standard reply. "You never know what you might miss." Many Chargers fans likely rued their early exit from the stadium on Nov. 22, 1998, when the Chargers scored three touchdowns in the last eight minutes to stun the Chiefs, 38-37. My friend Lauri Lockwood, who worked at *The Californian*, a sister paper of the *North County Times*, and I were definitely glad we stayed till the end.

5. It's Flutie Time. Oct. 28, 2001: Bills vs. Chargers. Doug Flutie led the Chargers to a 27-24 comeback win over the Bills, his most recent former team. Almost sacked at the 20-yard line, he managed to slip away and run the ball in for the winning score with about a minute to play. I loved to watch Flutie play. He was one of those athletes who could make you believe that anything was possible so long as there was time left on the clock.

4. Powder Blues and Bambi. Nov. 20, 2005: Bills vs. Chargers. Just days before Thanksgiving, Drew Brees carved up the Bills' defense, completing 28 of 33 passes for 339 yards and four TDs in a 48-10 triumph, which incidentally was my 200th NFL game. Brees and his teammates not only played well, they looked great, too, in their throwback powder blue uniforms, evoking memories of the Chargers' days in the AFL. The retro look was all the more appropriate because on that day the team retired the No. 19 jersey of Pro Football Hall of Fame wide receiver Lance Alworth, nicknamed "Bambi" for his elusiveness.

I can't help but think of another Hall of Fame athlete who wore No. 19 for a San Diego franchise. I wasn't fortunate enough to see Lance Alworth play for the Chargers, but I was blessed to see Tony Gwynn play 20 years for the Friars. Rest in peace, Mr. Padre. You left this world much too soon.

3. The Greatness of LT. Dec. 10, 2006: Broncos vs. Chargers. Every now and then there comes along a player whose ability tilts the field decidedly in his team's favor. LaDainian Tomlinson was one such player. He was so much fun to watch play. Anywhere he was on the field, he could take it the distance.

Or he could suddenly pull up and catch the defense flat-footed with a perfect pass to an open receiver. This game marked the zenith of his career, as he broke the single-season touchdown record. Later that year, he broke the record for points in a season, a mark held for more than 45 years by Pro Football Hall of Famer Paul Hornung. Soon thereafter, Tomlinson was named league MVP, an award usually bestowed on quarterbacks.

2. The Most Painful Loss. Jan. 14, 2007: Patriots vs. Chargers. This was supposed to be the time when all the stars were aligned for the Bolts: A 14-2 record, led by the Coach of the Year and the league's MVP. Alas, fate turned a potential game-clinching interception into a lost fumble that gave Tom Brady and Co. one more chance to win. Rubbing even more salt into the wound? The fumble was recovered by former Chargers wide receiver Reche Caldwell, who then caught a TD pass and later a 49-yard pass to set up the winning score.

Even though the Chargers lost this game, I gained an immeasurable amount of respect for Philip Rivers near the end of it. He raced his teammates down the field in the last seconds to give the Chargers a chance to tie the game with a field goal and send it into overtime. Nate Kaeding's 54-yard attempt fell short, but Rivers' effort didn't. He gave everything he could on the field that day and every other time I saw him play, just like Dan Marino.

The emotions of that day were aptly summed up by a photograph I took soon after the game of the two people who joined me for it. My friend Sabrina Prestigiacomo, like me a Bolts backer then, put on a brave face, which contrasted with the beaming smile of my friend and NCT colleague Amanda Selvidio. She's a Rhode Island native and fan of the New England sports triumvirate (Celtics, Patriots, Red Sox). As disappointed as I was for Sabrina and myself, I was happy for Amanda that she got to see firsthand an incredible victory for her team.

1. San Diego Super Chargers! Jan. 2, 2009: Colts vs. Chargers. Aside from seeing Bob Griese lead the Dolphins to victory here in 1978, this game was the best time I ever had at the Murph. Watching the Bolts prevail over future Hall of Famer Peyton Manning and the Colts in a playoff game, in sudden-death overtime, no less, was electrifying beyond words. Seeing Darren Sproles cross that goal line for the winning score was as good as it ever got for this San Diego Chargers fan.

Attending the game with me was a friend of mine from high school, Sean Bohan, a Chargers fan seemingly since birth who incidentally took me to that OT thriller against the Raiders in 1985. It wasn't easy being a Dolphins fan in San Diego during the Air Coryell era, especially since the Bolts usually came out on top in those matchups, winning four of six. After Dan Marino retired in March 2000, I switched allegiances to my hometown team. Sean and I were now on the same page as far as the NFL was concerned. Sharing this special moment with him after all our rivalry games added another layer of enjoyment to this Chargers victory for me.

Honorable mention No. 1: Super Bowl XXXVII: The Bucs Romp Here. Jan. 27, 2003. It cost me $1,675 to see this game, my first Super Bowl. The amount I paid to get in was more than four times the face value of my ticket, $400, but believe me I got my money's worth. It may not have been a very competitive game, but there were still great plays made by players on both sides, including touchdowns by future Hall of Famers Jerry Rice (for Oakland) and Derrick Brooks (for Tampa Bay).

Throw in the musical acts that performed before, during or after the game (Santana with Michelle Branch, Celine Dion, The Dixie Chicks, Shania Twain, No Doubt, Sting and Bon Jovi) and the $200 tip I got from Buccaneers fans for giving them a lift to their hotel after the game, I'd say I had a Super day!

Honorable mention No. 2: Jan. 1, 2017: Chiefs vs. Chargers. Nearly eight years to the day I saw my most memorable Chargers game here, I saw my last one. The Bolts lost 37-27 to Kansas City. The game had the feeling of a wake, as most Chargers fans, myself included, feared that this truly would be the Bolts' final game as the home team in San Diego. Eleven days later came the official announcement that the team was indeed leaving town.

One historic moment Chargers fans hoped to see before the team left town was tight end Antonio Gates breaking Tony Gonzalez's record for most TDs by a tight end in NFL history. He needed two TDs that day to do so. Unfortunately, he could only get one to tie. Gates was blanketed by the Chiefs' defense, so QB Philip Rivers had little choice but to throw to Hunter Henry, Chargers' other tight end on the field, for a TD late in the game. It was the last one the Bolts would score as San Diego's NFL team, and more significantly, the city's first major pro sports franchise.

I'm thankful my friend, NCT colleague and die-hard Chiefs fan Monica Hodes-Smail and her husband, Eric Smail, joined me for this game. It was tough knowing that I might never again experience the NFL in my hometown. If this was my last NFL game in America's Finest City, I'm glad it was with two people who were representative of the friends and family members who attended games with me: Passionate but never boorish about the Chargers or the visiting team and respectful of the fans around us.

I was deeply saddened but not surprised when the San Diego Chargers decided to move to Los Angeles. Much has been said and written about that decision, so I won't add much more to it. But I'll always believe that a deal could have and should have been reached to the satisfaction of the NFL, the Chargers and the city of San Diego to build a new stadium in Mission Valley.

Thanks for the memories, Murph!

Post-500 commentary: SDCCU Stadium was razed in 2020 to make room for Aztecs Stadium, a 35,000-seat stadium slated to open in September 2022. Although the San Diego State University

Aztecs football team will be the venue's primary tenant, the facility can be expanded to 55,000 seats if the NFL wishes to return to America's Finest City. If that ever happens, and the facility has the prerequisite grass field, you can be sure I'll be among the first in line for season tickets.

CHAPTER TWENTY-SIX
HALLOWED GROUND
FOR DOLPHINS FANS

Los Angeles Memorial Coliseum	Los Angeles, CA
Games Seen There: 20	*First Game: Oct. 9, 1988*
	Last Game: Dec. 29, 2019

There's no stadium in the U.S. that can match the L.A. Coliseum when it comes to hosting historic sporting events. Among them, two Olympic Games (with a third on the horizon) and two Super Bowls, including the inaugural game in 1967.

As for NFL football, it's hallowed ground for people like me who grew up Miami Dolphins fans in the 1970s. This is where the dream of perfection was realized with a victory in Super Bowl VII. I wasn't fortunate enough to see that event in person, but I still witnessed a significant moment in that team's history when I saw my first NFL game outside of San Diego with my friend Kurt Rowland as we watched the Dolphins battle the Raiders here in 1988.

It was 104 degrees at kickoff, likely the warmest game I've ever attended. I hope so. I have no desire to ever break that record.

The first half was everything I could have hoped for, as the Dolphins scored 24 points in the second quarter, then held on for a 24-14 win, their first ever over the Raiders on the West Coast, ending a streak of nine straight losses. I brought a little stuffed dolphin with me to the game in L.A. for luck. Looks like it worked.

Skip ahead five years, and I'm here for a Chargers-Raiders

game, my first road trip via a travel agency. We took a bus up to the Coliseum and received quite a welcome upon entering the parking lot. Our bus was pelted with a pumpkin; it was Halloween after all. That made for both a festive and ghoulish atmosphere.

The game between the Chargers and Raiders was tied at 17 in the third quarter when Raiders QB Jeff Hostetler aimed a pass to the end zone for future Hall of Fame wide receiver Tim Brown. It never reached him. Instead, Donald Frank of the Chargers stepped in front of him and went coast to coast with it, 102 yards for the go-ahead score. My fellow Chargers fans and I, including my friend Jeff Darby, immediately started singing the chant we'd heard from Raiders fans whenever they'd scored that day. "Whoomp (There It Is)." We had a very happy bus ride back down to San Diego, as the Chargers won 30-23.

A special word of thanks to Jeff and his brother John Darby. Jeff has helped me attend NFL games all over the U.S., from Oakland to Houston to Baltimore, while John, an executive with ScooterBug, has had technicians Armando Briseno and Reggie Wilson give my well-traveled wheelchair, which I've used for 400-plus NFL games, a tune-up every summer so it's ready to withstand the rigors of the NFL season. Thanks, guys!

When the Rams announced in 2016 that they would take up residency here again, albeit temporarily until their new stadium in Inglewood was completed, I jumped at the chance to attend more games here. Seemingly popping up like a lucky penny, my first game back here after a 23-year hiatus featured the Rams playing the Dolphins. Once more, I got to see the Dolphins play at the scene of the franchise's greatest triumph.

The game may have been played in traditionally sunny Southern California, but it was a very soggy day. Miami was able to snatch the game away from Los Angeles with two touchdowns in the final four minutes of the contest to win 14-10, the same number of points they scored on that field to achieve perfection 44 years earlier.

Joining me for this contest was Tom Graves, one of my colleagues at Sun Newspapers. Tom, like many people who've joined me for games, was attending his first one. I must confess I get a big kick out of introducing friends and relatives to the excitement that is live NFL football.

Post 500 commentary: Following the 2017 season, I let my Los Angeles Chargers season ticket expire and signed up for season tickets with the Rams for the next two seasons. I saw some great football, as the Rams went 11-3 in home games I attended, including a win over Aaron Rodgers and the Packers, two victories over Russell Wilson and the Seattle Seahawks and a divisional playoff game triumph in January 2019 against the Dallas Cowboys en route to a berth in Super Bowl LIII.

Also included among those 14 games was one I call "The Track Meet at the Coliseum." The game between the Chiefs and the Rams on Nov. 19, 2018, wasn't even supposed to be played there. It had been scheduled for Mexico City but was moved to Los Angeles due to poor field conditions at Azteca Stadium.

It was the football equivalent of an Ali-Frazier fight, as both teams traded scoring blows, on offense and on defense. The Rams finally prevailed, outlasting the Chiefs and their wunderkind QB, Patrick Mahomes, 54-51. It's without question one of the greatest NFL games I've seen live, and the most unforgettable regular-season game I've ever witnessed.

I also saw the historic Los Angeles Memorial Coliseum undergo an impressive renovation that should keep it among the top sports venues for decades to come.

Something else very modern when it comes to the L.A. Coliseum: the convenience of mass transit. For many of the NFL games I saw there last decade I had a familiar routine: drive to the Oceanside Transit Center, take the Orange County Transportation Authority's Metrolink train from there to L.A. Union Station, transfer there to

Metro 7th Street Station, then a quick ride on one more Metro train and you're within easy walking distance (or rolling distance if you use a wheelchair like me) to the Coliseum.

All in all, it's a great way to avoid the gridlock that is L.A. traffic, especially on game day. And I can still follow that route if I ever go to a USC game. If my alma mater, San Diego State University, plays the Trojans there again I definitely will.

One game for which the train was not an option for me was the Buccaneers-Rams game in 2019. That day I was eight days removed from having emergency gallbladder surgery and not up to riding the rails. I needed a direct trip to and from the game. Thanks to Marwan Razouk, another former NCT colleague of mine who was gracious enough to help me out, he got to see his first NFL game at the L.A. Coliseum, and I got to witness another track meet there, this time with a total of 95 points scored.

Unlike the one between the Chiefs and Rams the year before, though, this was no photo finish. Final score: Buccaneers 55, Rams 40.

My most recent NFL game here, the 205th and perhaps final one in SoCal for me, with Sofi Stadium and its artificial surface now the sole home for NFL action in the region, was a low-key but still memorable one between the Cardinals and Rams. Not only did the Rams give me a pleasant, if wistful memory with a 31-24 victory, I got to share the fun with a new member of my family, Mykell Engesath, husband of my niece Keely. It was his first NFL game. To have it take place at such an historic venue when it's likely hosting its last such event, that's what I call timing!

And among the highlights of attending a game in a sports venue in L.A. is seeing what stars are sitting among you in the crowd. Among the luminaries I've seen on the Coliseum video board at NFL games are actors Danny Trejo and Rob Lowe. The night I saw Lowe, he was wearing a Leo Farnsworth jersey from the movie "Heaven Can Wait." That just seemed so right, because scenes from that Warren

Beatty movie were filmed there.

Last, but not least, I saw one Rams superfan of note recognized on the playing field itself. I may betray my age when I reveal the name of this former superstar, but I don't care. Peace, love and Bobby Sherman, everyone!

CHAPTER TWENTY-SEVEN
NEARLY A PERFECT FIT

Levi's Stadium	Santa Clara, CA
Games Seen There: 16	First Game: Nov. 2, 2014
	Last Game: Oct. 3, 2021

Much has been written about the unforgiving heat at this venue if your seats, like mine, have the sun shining on them. While I'm no fan of weather extremes, hot or cold, I'm more than willing to put up with a little discomfort for 49ers home games here because the game-day experience is so much easier than the logistical nightmare that was getting in and out of Candlestick Park.

Here, all I do is get on a light-rail line just steps from my hotel, and before I know it, I'm at the stadium. And the ride back is just as easy.

The stadium itself, sans Mother Nature's heat lamp, is also a nice upgrade from my viewing experience at Candlestick. Here, I don't have to worry about someone walking or standing in front of me at an inopportune moment.

As for the games I've seen here, the one that stands out most was a Saturday night game against the San Diego Chargers, Dec. 20, 2014. As it was just five days before Christmas, I brought a Santa cap featuring Chargers colors with me. I made sure to put it on once the game began for luck. At first, the luck was all bad, with the 49ers up 28-7 at halftime.

After that, though, the Chargers permitted just one more score by the 49ers, an amazing 90-yard run by quarterback Colin Kaepernick.

It missed breaking the record for longest TD run by a QB by just three yards. That mark was set the year before on the other side of the Bay Area by Terrelle Pryor, and I was lucky enough to witness that play firsthand as well.

The Chargers' defense didn't just hold the 49ers to one TD in the second half, it contributed one of its own on a fumble recovery by Corey Liuget in the third quarter. Add three touchdown passes by Philip Rivers, the last one coming on a drive with two clutch fourth-down completions, and to overtime we went.

The 49ers won the coin toss and were driving for the winning score when the Chargers' perennial Pro Bowl safety, Eric Weddle, forced a fumble recovered by the Bolts. Soon, Rivers and Co. set up kicker Nick Novak for the winning field goal.

I wasn't comfortable wearing that Santa cap before the game, but afterward, I was beaming with pride while sporting it. And why not? For this then-Chargers fan, Christmas came early that year.

Following my 500th game at Lambeau Field, I knew exactly where I wanted to see my next NFL game, No. 501. Levi's Stadium, of course! I even bought myself a pair of the iconic jeans and wore them to the stadium. It seemed to work, too. The 49ers won that day, beating the Giants 31-21. I also got to visit with my friend Kip Kuduk, my companion for Super Bowl XLIX, who was there cheering on his beloved Giants.

Just as I was fortunate to be a season-ticket holder with the Rams during the 2018 season, which saw them reach the Super Bowl, I was able to see the 49ers reach the following Super Bowl as a season-ticket holder as well. And with the NFC's best record, I got to attend both playoff victories, first against the Vikings and then the Packers.

CHAPTER TWENTY-EIGHT
CARSON'S FINE,
BUT IT AIN'T HOME

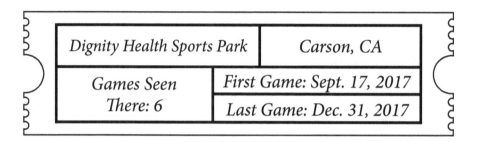

Dignity Health Sports Park	Carson, CA
Games Seen There: 6	First Game: Sept. 17, 2017
	Last Game: Dec. 31, 2017

I decided to renew my season tickets with the Chargers after the team moved north, not out of loyalty, but curiosity. I was intrigued by what it would be like to see NFL games in such a small, but well-maintained venue. And since it sported the necessary grass field, I felt obliged to at least see a few games here that would also help me reach my goal of seeing ny 500th one in 2017 in Green Bay before wintry weather arrived there.

The experiences I had at the games I attended here were a mix of emotions for me. The view from my seat was good, though I missed having the perspective from higher up that I had gotten so used to from dozens of Chargers home games at the Murph. Then there was the matter of seeing the same Chargers players, especially Philip Rivers and Antonio Gates, wearing the same colors but now representing Los Angeles.

I decided before the season started that the Rams and Chiefs would be my new favorite teams. I would no longer root for the Chargers, but would be happy for Gates and Rivers in whatever future success they may have. I must have looked like a Vulcan at these games, expressing hardly any emotion outwardly but being a jumble of nerves on the inside, especially when the Chargers played the Chiefs, old favorite team versus new one.

Every time there's a new chapter in my football travels, it seems to be a game involving the Dolphins. That was the case again on Sept. 17, 2017, as once again the Dolphins intersected with my itinerary. Two moments that really stand out for me from this game were Antonio Gates setting the record for most TD receptions by a tight end, for which I respectfully cheered, and the missed field goal attempt by the Chargers with five seconds left in the contest. I offered no visible opinion on that play.

Despite the miss, the team's celebratory cannon was inexplicably fired, which I think was a perfect metaphor for the end of this relocation saga. Time will tell if the Chargers' return to the Los Angeles area was a misfire by the team. I just hope the NFL comes back to San Diego someday. If that happens, and the team will be playing its home games on a grass field, I'll be among the first in line for season tickets.

CHAPTER TWENTY-NINE
THE AGONY & THE ECSTASY

State Farm Stadium	Glendale, AZ
Games Seen There: 39	First Game: Sept. 10, 2006
	Last Game: Oct. 28, 2021

This venue is without a doubt the best one with a grass field in the NFL. It's climate-controlled, so you escape the desert heat the moment you get inside. And the way so much light comes into the place even when the roof is closed is fantastic. It doesn't have a warehouse feel, which some other sports structures with retractable roofs do.

This stadium has played host to two of the most unforgettable Super Bowls. I was fated to be here for both of them, I only wish I'd had a fan of the winning team with me.

After attending Super Bowl XXXVII in San Diego in 2003, I reveled in what a wonderful time I had at the game but lamented that I wasn't able to share the experience with someone I knew.

Fast-forward to 2007. Thanks to the assistance of an anonymous friend, I was given the opportunity to buy two tickets at face value to Super Bowl XLII. One of my colleagues at the *North County Times* newspaper, Amanda Selvidio, is a fan of the Patriots, who were pursuing an undefeated season. So when I got the tickets in December, I invited her to the game and she accepted.

Ironically my favorite team then, the Chargers, had a chance to spoil New England's date with destiny in the AFC Championship

Game but that was not to be, so I went in wholeheartedly for the Patriots in Super Bowl XLII, hoping that Amanda and I would witness firsthand a championship game that would be talked about for years. We got that, but not with the result we wanted. I felt so badly for Amanda that her team had come up just short in its pursuit of perfection, losing 17-14 to the New York Giants.

I needn't have worried about her, though. She was disappointed but hardly crushed by the outcome. It turns out her dad is a Giants fan!

Skip ahead seven years, and the Super Bowl is back in Glendale. The Patriots are back as well, not pursuing perfection this time, just seeking to beat the Seahawks and win another Super Bowl after two losses in the Big Game to the Giants (XLII, XLVI).

Before the NFL season began, I asked my friend Kip Kuduk, the die-hard Giants fan and ex-NCT colleague who had just moved to the Phoenix area, if he'd like to see the game should I get my name picked in the NFL's annual ADA Super Bowl drawing. He said yes, and offered to provide me a place to stay should we get tickets. Luck was on our side, as mine was one of the winning entries, which meant we could buy our tickets at face value, $800 apiece.

Before the game, I gave Kip my Super Bowl XLII hat and T-shirt. I figure he would enjoy them a lot more than I had.

As for Super Bowl XLIX, it was a very exciting game, with the Patriots scoring two TDs in the fourth quarter, to overcome a 10-point deficit and take the lead. Then it seemed the football gods were going to once again let victory be snatched away from New England. Jermaine Kearse, like David Tyree seven years before him, made an improbable catch that put the Seahawks on the doorstep of victory and a second consecutive Super Bowl win.

Kip and I had a perfect view of the play and what happened moments later as New England cornerback Malcolm Butler anticipated a slant pass and beat Seahawks receiver Ricardo Lockette to the ball at the goal line to seal the win for the Patriots. The crowd in the stadium was stunned into silence. Then we heard elation from Patriots fans and sounds of disbelief from Seahawks supporters.

As for Amanda, immediately after the game I sent her a text noting how the Patriots were Super Bowl champs once again and later gave her a picture of the scoreboard saluting them as such.

If I ever get my hands on a DeLorean with a flux capacitor, the first thing I'll do is go back in time and take Kip to Super Bowl XLII and Amanda to Super Bowl XLIX.

I've been lucky enough to see four other notable games here, all involving the primary tenant, the Arizona Cardinals. Three of them were postseason affairs, including the 2008 NFC Championship Game against the Eagles. Kurt Warner, continuing the career renaissance that led to his induction to the Pro Football Hall of Fame, led Arizona to a 32-25 victory over Philadelphia and the franchise's first Super Bowl berth.

The next playoff game here, in January 2010, was a wild-card matchup between the Packers and the Cardinals. Wild was indeed the operative word, as the game set a postseason record for most total points scored, 96. Together, Kurt Warner and Aaron Rodgers threw for nine touchdowns and 802 yards.

The game actually was won on a defensive play early in overtime. My sister Kitty and I were in prime viewing position in the upper deck for the winning play. We were happy the home team won, but something seemed off about it. Instant replay confirmed our suspicions. When forcing the fumble by Aaron Rodgers that Karlos Dansby then cradled and took in for the winning score, Arizona defender Michael Adams clearly grabbed hold of Rodgers' facemask. A 15-yard penalty nullifying the touchdown should have been called, but wasn't.

The game was part of a memorable sports weekend for Kitty and me. The next day, we saw one of her favorite teams play, the Phoenix Suns. Future Basketball Hall of Famer Steve Nash scored 30 points in a 105-101 victory over the Milwaukee Bucks. Basketball is not a favorite sport of mine, as I rank it fourth behind hockey among the major ones in the U.S. Still, I always enjoy watching great athletes no matter the field of competition.

The Packers and Cardinals met again in the postseason in January 2016, when Rodgers completed not one but two Hail Mary passes to enable the Packers to tie the game with no time left in regulation and send it to overtime. My friend Jacob Pomrenke, a former NCT colleague and die-hard Packers fan, joined me for this game.

Unfortunately for Rodgers, Green Bay never got the ball back. Another Canton-bound player, Arizona wide receiver Larry Fitzgerald, put on his own display of postseason thrills with a 75-yard catch and run on the first play from scrimmage in overtime, followed by a 5-yard TD reception from Carson Palmer to win the game.

Last, but certainly not least, was a regular-season game I saw here in 2006 between the Cardinals and their former Windy City neighbors, the Bears. The game itself, a nail-biting 24-23 win by Chicago, was overshadowed by Cardinals coach Dennis Green's postgame press conference, which ended with the terse line: "They (the Bears) are who we thought they were. And we let them off the hook!"

I heard that line in a taxi on the way back to my hotel that night. It was an unforgettable moment to be sure, but it saddens me that people these days when they think of Dennis Green are more apt to think of this tirade than the fact he was a good head coach who mentored a lot of able assistants who went on to become successful head coaches in their own right, including Super Bowl winners Brian Billick and Tony Dungy.

I can't end this chapter about my NFL adventures in Arizona without mentioning my good friends Jeanelle Cabello and Nahshon Menefee. They helped me out in a time of need one year when I had my two season tickets but no ride to a Cardinals game. Jeanelle was working at the hotel I was staying at that weekend and let her husband, Nahshon, know of my predicament. He and I ended up going to that game together and as a result, I got to know them both well.

The three of us now attend one Cardinals game per year together, and it's among the games I most look forward to attending each season.

Post-500 commentary: It took 526 games, but it finally happened. I saw my first tie game on Sept. 8, 2019, when the Lions and Cardinals deadlocked at 27. It was surreal afterward. Fans of both teams seemed to be in a daze, unsure how to react to a tie score. There was none of the typical postgame hooting and hollering echoing through the concourses as fans walked out. It was a scene I'll never forget.

CHAPTER THIRTY
HANG ON, BROWNS FANS,
BROWNS FANS HANG ON

FirstEnergy Stadium	Cleveland, OH
Games Seen There: 18	*First Game: Oct. 7, 2001*
	Last Game: Sept. 26, 2021

Of the 18 NFL games I've witnessed here, five are especially memorable: three impressive victories and two disappointing losses.

Seahawks-Browns 2007: Phil Dawson's 25-yard field goal gives the Browns the winning margin in overtime, 33-30, in a classic seesaw game where the teams traded scores six times in the third and fourth quarter. Running back Jamal Lewis scored four TDs on the ground for Cleveland.

Ravens-Browns 2009: The Browns were clearly unprepared for their close-up in this nationally televised game I attended with my cousin Tom Opincar. Cleveland's offense was colder than the 30-degree wind chill, accumulating just 160 yards in a 16-0 loss to Baltimore. A sign displayed by one person at the game, which was shown in *The Plain Dealer* newspaper the next day, read: "Hey Baltimore, Can You Take This Team, Too?" a pointed reference to Art Modell's move of the original Browns to that city after the 1995 season.

Rams-Browns 2011: I chose to attend this game because I thought it would be fun to see the Rams play in their ancestral home. What I got was an ending that had to be seen to be believed. With a little more than two minutes left in the game, Dawson lined up to try a chip-shot 27-yard field goal. The snap from center was bounced, causing the football to roll instead of fly back to the holder. This threw off Dawson's timing as he pulled his kick wide, which enabled the Rams to run out the clock and escape with a one-point win.

Bills-Browns 2013: With NFL legend Jim Brown looking on after having his name placed in the stadium's Ring of Honor, the Browns scored an impressive win in a Thursday night game in early October, scoring the final 20 points of the contest. It was a costly victory, though, as QB Brian Hoyer, who grew up in Cleveland, was injured early in the first quarter, lost for the season with a torn ACL.

Travis Benjamin gave Cleveland its first lead with a 79-yard punt return. It seemed more like a 130-yard return, as Benjamin ran nearly the entire width of the field while dipping and dodging Buffalo defenders. T.J. Ward iced the victory for the Browns with a 44-yard pick-six in the fourth quarter.

Steelers-Browns 2014: I attended my first Steelers-Browns game in Cleveland and saw the Browns crush the Steelers 31-10. Special thanks to my friend Dave Brown, another *North County Times* alum, and die-hard Steelers fan, who helped me get to this game and willingly endured lots of trash talk without responding in kind.

Even though it hasn't been the site of a lot of great football games since it opened in 2001, FirstEnergy Stadium is one of the best venues in the league. The atmosphere is great, and the pageantry before the game is always fun, as is the fans singing along to "Hang On Sloopy" after the end of the third quarter, which includes spelling out "Ohio." The Browns are truly headed in the right direction with the drafting of Baker Mayfield and other personnel moves. There's no more devoted fan base in the NFL.

The reason I've been able to see so many games in this stadium is thanks to my many relatives in the Cleveland area who have joined me for several of them, cousins Tom and Tim Opincar, Tim's sons Jake and Alex, and particularly my uncle, Bruce Reiman. His family had season tickets from the team's founding in 1946 through 1995, ending only with the move to Baltimore. He was at the first game on ABC's "Monday Night Football" when the Browns hosted the Jets, and many other Browns home games from the 1960s into the 1990s until owner Art Modell moved the franchise to Baltimore and rebranded them as the Ravens.

Post-500 commentary: My Uncle Bruce and I saw the Browns battle the Chiefs here in early November 2018, the day after I dropped off my 500-plus ticket collection at the Pro Football Hall of Fame. The Browns fought gamely but were still outclassed by the Chiefs. The headline in *The Plain Dealer* the next day was memorable: Hail to the Chiefs.

CHAPTER THIRTY-ONE
BEAR DOWN, CHICAGO BEARS

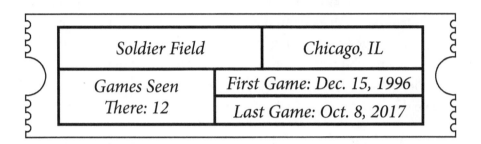

Soldier Field	Chicago, IL
Games Seen There: 12	First Game: Dec. 15, 1996
	Last Game: Oct. 8, 2017

Chicago is a city you can't visit often enough. I love coming here for Bears games, though the spaceship parked on Soldier Field as part of the early 2000s renovation has taken me a long time to get used to. I actually preferred the original look of the stadium, which had qualified for designation as a national historic landmark. That honor was stripped away after the renovation. At least they had the good sense to keep the grass field.

As for the game experience here, I always love seeing the Bears score, because then I know the crowd will soon be singing "Bear Down, Chicago Bears," a fight song written in 1941 that praises the team's adoption of the T formation, which revolutionized the game.

And a thank you to the Bears, for serving RC Cola. I hadn't enjoyed that drink in years until I saw it being sold at Bears games last decade.

As for the games I've attended here, three stand out for various reasons.

Lions-Bears 2010: Much of the polarizing debate over what constitutes a catch spring from a deciding play in this game. I thought then, and still do, that Calvin Johnson made a touchdown catch with

24 seconds left. It was indeed originally ruled a touchdown. Then it was overturned on replay review. It should have given the Lions the lead. Instead, Detroit lost, 19-14. Given how the NFL recently revised once more its rule on what constitutes a catch, I think that TD would be upheld today.

Packers-Bears 2010: This was my first time seeing these foes play each other, the 180th game in the oldest rivalry in the NFL. It was a very exciting back-and-forth game which included a 62-yard punt return for a touchdown by the ever-elusive Devon Hester. Jay Cutler was able to outduel Aaron Rodgers and lead the Bears to the winning field goal by Robbie Gould with four seconds left.

Vikings-Bears 2017: While the Bears did lose this game, it's notable for being the first game QB Mitchell Trubisky started in the NFL. He proceeded to not only complete his first TD pass but followed it up by running the ball in the end zone on a trick-play two-point conversion to tie the game. The Vikings eventually won, 20-17, I also saw something I'd never seen before, when Bears punter Pat O'Donnell completed a touchdown pass to running back Benny Cunningham.

This chapter wouldn't be complete without a few words of appreciation for my Chicago friends, the Latasiewicz family, whom I've been blessed to know for more than 30 years. Their son Jay was one of the bus drivers who helped me get to and from San Diego State University when I was a student there. He made it possible for me and my friend Kurt Rowland to stay in the Second City with his parents Doris and Leo and twin sisters Jill and Jan, during my first trip there in 1985. Since then, they have helped me attend Cubs, White Sox and Bears games over the years, and even a Cardinals baseball game in St. Louis in 2000.

I cannot thank the Latasiewiczs enough for the kindness and generosity they've shown me. After my first game at Soldier Field in 1996, I had a chance to see Michael Jordan and the Bulls play that evening at the United Center. I passed it up so I could have dinner with them and congratulate daughters Jill Latasiewicz Laramie and Jan Latasiewicz Anderson who had both gotten married recently.

CHAPTER THIRTY-TWO
THE PRODIGAL STADIUM

M&T Bank Stadium	Baltimore, MD
Games Seen There: 6	First Game: Oct. 21, 1997
	Last Game: Oct. 15, 2017

The second game I saw here turned out to be a festive moment for the Ravens. Head coach Brian Billick had forbidden any use of the word "playoffs" by anyone affiliated with the team, so when it clinched a spot in the Super Bowl tournament with a dominating 24-3 win over the Chargers in December 2000, "Festivus" became the operative word when discussing the playoffs.

Zoom ahead 15 years, and now I'm the one in a festive mood. In December 2015, the Ravens announced that they would be taking out the artificial turf field at M&T Bank Stadium and going back to a natural grass playing surface for the 2016 season. I was beside myself with joy when I heard this news, as I'd really enjoyed my four previous visits there.

Immediately I texted my friend and former *North County Times* colleague Jaime Bowden and asked her if she'd like to join me for a game in Baltimore sometime the following year. She agreed at once, noting that Baltimore was just 90 minutes from where she lives in West Virginia.

M&T Bank is currently the only NFL venue to start with a grass field, switch to an artificial surface, and then go back to grass. I'm still holding out hope that one day Gillette Stadium, NRG Stadium, Bank of America Stadium and/or Paul Brown Stadium may return to their natural roots, too.

As for memorable games here, I have two favorites and one honorable mention.

Steelers-Ravens 2002: This was not a close game, as Pittsburgh took control early en route to a 31-18 victory. Still what made it memorable was it was Game 1 of my first-ever NFL doubleheader. After this game, my friend Giovanni Prestigiacomo and I drove 32 miles to FedEx Field to see the Indianapolis Colts play Washington in Game 2.

Little did I realize it would be my last game in Baltimore for 14 years, as the Ravens installed an artificial surface the following spring.

Bears-Ravens 2017: My most recent game here, this one was quite exciting, needing overtime to decide a winner: Bears 27 Ravens 24. I felt so bad for the Ravens that they lost that day, especially after they had tied the score on an electrifying 77-yard punt return by Michael Campanaro and a two-point conversion via a one-handed catch by tight end Nick Boyle.

Honorable mention: What else? Browns-Ravens Nov. 11, 2016. Returning to this stadium for an NFL game after a 14-year hiatus was one of the biggest highlights of my quest to 500 games. It didn't matter that the game that night wasn't very competitive (Ravens 28, Browns 7). Coming back to one of my favorite venues for an NFL game made this game truly memorable.

Special thanks to Ravens officials Gwen Sieck and Elli Peltonen, who, in addition to helping me secure ADA seating here, upon learning of my quest to see 500 games, made me feel very welcome by presenting me with team souvenirs. I definitely hope to make it to double digits in games here in the near future.

Post-500 commentary: True to my word, I'm trying to see more Ravens games here. I had tickets to their game against the Cowboys in December 2020, but the COVID-19 pandemic scuttled those plans. I'm hoping to make it to a game here in 2021, Vikings vs. Ravens. I chose this one in tribute to my late mother, who loved the color purple.

CHAPTER THIRTY-THREE
WHAT'S IN A NAME?

Nissan Stadium	Nashville, TN
Games Seen There: 6	First Game: Dec. 9, 1999
	Last Game: Oct. 16, 2017

It seems that nearly every time I attend a Titans home game, the venue has a new name. Not just a new sponsor in the title, but also another descriptive term for the building. First it was Adelphia Coliseum, then LP Field and now Nissan Stadium. I don't know what company will be the next sponsor, but I'm guessing the rest of the structure's name will be Polo Grounds.

As for the games I've seen here, four stand out in my mind.

Raiders-Titans 1999: This was my first game in this stadium and the first prime-time NFL game in the state of Tennessee. Wynonna Judd sang the national anthem before the game. As she finished the song, she took off her coat, revealing a Titans jersey underneath.

The Titans' offense that night was all Eddie George. The former Ohio State star and Heisman Trophy winner ran for 199 yards and two touchdowns in leading the Titans to a 21-14 win over Jon Gruden and the Oakland Raiders. Special thanks to former *North County Times* alum and Tennessee native Nancy Tucker DeGennaro, who not only joined me for the game but also gave me a quick tour of nearby landmarks, including the famed replica of the Parthenon.

Browns-Titans 2008: If I was to sum this game up in one word, it would be "COLD." The temperature was 32 degrees at kickoff with a wind chill of 26 degrees, according to ProFootballReference.com. To make things even worse, I was sitting in the shade. I was pulling for the Browns that day, but even their quick 6-0 lead failed to warm me up. Eventually the Titans took control of the game and won going away, 28-9.

After the game, I took refuge in the Hard Rock Cafe and had a hot meal to fill me up and also help me defrost until I was able to take a cab back to my hotel.

Steelers-Titans 2012: This was another highly entertaining prime-time game. Scoring-wise it was mostly a battle of the two teams' placekickers who together made seven field goals in the contest. With the score tied at 23 late in the fourth quarter, Steelers placekicker Shaun Suisham came up one yard short on his 54-yard field goal attempt, while his Titans counterpart Rob Bironas drilled a 40-yarder through the uprights as time expired, giving Tennessee the 26-23 win.

Chargers-Titans 2013: Singer Amy Grant performed several tunes during pregame ceremonies, much to my delight. This was my second straight Chargers road game. I had been in Philadelphia the week before and saw them beat the Eagles on a last-second field goal and hoped for another road win in Nashville.

Unfortunately, it wasn't meant to be, as the Titans won on a 94-yard TD drive in the last two minutes. It included a tipped pass that was held ever so briefly by a Chargers defender, before it was jarred loose by a near-simultaneous collision with a Titans player.

While I'm not able to make it to Nashville often for Titans games, when I do, I usually get an exciting one. This is one place I definitely hope to visit again no matter what they call it.

CHAPTER THIRTY-FOUR
THANKS, OLD FRIEND

Oakland-Alameda County Coliseum	Oakland, CA
Games Seen There: 71	First Game: Sept. 3, 1995
	Last Game: Dec. 15, 2019

If you had told me as a child that I would someday wax nostalgic about the Oakland-Alameda County Coliseum, I would have thought you were crazy. That was the site of the most painful loss I've ever felt in all my years of watching football, either on TV or in person, the "Sea of Hands" game where the Raiders beat the Dolphins in the first round of the 1974 playoffs, denying them the chance to be the first team to win three consecutive Super Bowls.

And yet, 47 years later, I love the place, even if it is on its last legs. Part of those good vibes stem from just how easy it is to get to and from this place, unlike its former Bay Area counterpart, Candlestick Park.

Most of the hotels in the vicinity of the Coliseum offer free shuttles to and from the Coliseum BART Station, part of the Bay Area's light-rail network. Once there, you go across a short walkway, and before you know it, you're at the Coliseum. It may take a little longer to reverse the process after the game, but it's still no morass, like heading to and leaving Candlestick Park.

Mostly, though, it's just knowing all the unforgettable games in pro football history that have taken place there: the Heidi Game, the Sea of Hands Game, the Patriots-Raiders playoff game in 1976 and so many more. Here are my favorite recollections of the Coliseum:

Chargers-Raiders 1995: There's no better place to start than here. My first Raiders game in Oakland was the team's first regular-season game there since returning to its ancestral home after spending 13 seasons in Los Angeles. This homecoming was truly a special day. I didn't even mind that the Raiders' victory that day came at the expense of my then-hometown San Diego Chargers (I was still a Dolphins fan then). Just seeing the renewal of the love affair between the Raiders and their Bay Area fans that day was worth the price of admission.

Dolphins-Raiders 1997: I consider this the bookend to Miami's victory in Los Angeles in 1988, the Dolphins' first win against the Raiders on the West Coast. With this 34-16 triumph, the Dolphins showed they could beat the Raiders in the Oakland Coliseum, too. How sweet it was to be there to witness that moment. It wasn't exactly revenge for the Sea of Hands Game, but I'll take it. Special thanks to my friend Jeff Darby for not only coming with me to the game, but making the long drive back and forth from San Diego that weekend.

Chiefs-Raiders 1998: This game, won by the Chiefs 31-24, was decided on a touchdown pass to future Pro Football Hall of Fame tight end Tony Gonzalez. Other eventual Hall of Famers linebacker Derrick Thomas and wide receiver Tim Brown also scored TDs, and cornerback Charles Woodson ended his rookie season by making his fifth interception. This game turned out to be Marty Schottenheimer's last one as the Chiefs head coach. Fittingly, it was against the Raiders, the team he dominated like no other, compiling an 18-3 record vs. them during his tenure in KC and 27-7 overall as an NFL head coach.

Packers-Raiders 2003: The day before this Monday night game, Brett Favre's father had died of a heart attack. Favre played that night and torched the Raiders' secondary for 311 yards and four TDs in the first half. The Packers went on to win 41-7. I've never seen a QB have a night like that. It seemed like every pass Favre threw that night, no matter how long the odds were, it would find its way to a Packers receiver. The headline in the Sports section of the *Oakland Tribune*, which I donated to the Hall of Fame in 2018, read: Mourning Glory.

My friend and former *North County Times* colleague Denis Devine not only joined me for this unforgettable game, he also treated me the night before to "The School of Rock," starring Jack Black, which was playing in theaters at the time. Such a fun movie. Thanks, Denis!

Twenty months after they met in Super Bowl XXXVII, the Raiders get a bit of revenge by beating Tampa Bay, 30-20. The Raiders led 30-6 before the Buccaneers got a couple late scores to make the final result appear more respectable. One of those scores was a 16-yard TD pass to Tim Brown, who had changed pirate ships before the start of the 2004 season. It was the 100th TD reception of his career. Even though Brown no longer wore Silver & Black, Raiders fans in the Coliseum heartily cheered the accomplishment when it was noted on the scoreboard.

Eagles-Raiders 2013: Four years before he led the Eagles to their first Super Bowl title, Nick Foles did something that only eight pro football signal-callers ever have done. He threw seven touchdown passes, needing just three quarters to reach that total as he led Philadelphia to a 49-20 win. Foles had a chance to break the record but wasn't able to move the football in his only series in the fourth quarter. He was then taken out of the game and relieved by Matt Barkley.

49ers-Raiders 2014: This was a fun rivalry game, made even more enjoyable because my younger brother Kevin came down from Petaluma to join me for it. Rookie QB Derek Carr had his best game of the season, throwing for 254 yards and three TDs on 22 of 28 passing, as Oakland prevailed over San Francisco 24-13.

Like all good rivalry games, there was a fair amount of support for the visitors in the stands, much more than usual at a Raiders game. Given that the Raiders no longer call the Bay Area home, I'm glad I saw their victorious swan song as the home team in this now-defunct NorCal series.

Chiefs-Raiders 2017: The 50th anniversary of the Raiders' first championship team was celebrated during this game and many of the surviving players were honored at halftime. As luck would have it, I stayed at the same hotel as many of them, and I had the distinct pleasure of meeting several of them, including the Mad Bomber himself, Daryle Lamonica. What a thrill!

Perhaps drawing inspiration from their forebears, the current Raiders squad went toe to toe with the rival Chiefs and won a hard-fought game, 31-30, on a last-second touchdown and extra point. And they did it wearing white at home with silver numbers, right up there with the Chargers' late 1960s powder blues as one of the best uniform combinations in football history.

Post-500 commentary: I can never say enough good things about my game-day experiences here, which numbered far more than any other venue outside San Diego. The ease with which I could get from my hotel to the game, the ability to get my favorite pizza, Round Table Pizza, before every game here, the passion of the fans for the Raiders, all the exciting plays I saw on the field, and the relative ease in which I could get back to my hotel. Ultimately, what I liked most was that the focus was always on football.

Given all that, I so hoped the Raiders would win their final game here in December 2019 and at least give their fans in the Bay Area a pleasant memory before moving away again. Unfortunately, the Jacksonville Jaguars scored the winning touchdown with 31 seconds left in the game, as the Coliseum sadly had no more football miracles left to give.

Still, the good times here far outnumbered the bad. Thank you, Oakland-Alameda County Coliseum! I hope the A's can get you another championship before the wrecking ball arrives.

CHAPTER THIRTY-FIVE
LET IT SNOW, LET IT SNOW
... 11-10?!

Heinz Field	Pittsburgh, PA
Games Seen There: 9	First Game: Oct. 29, 2001
	Last Game: Oct. 17, 2021

Like Raymond James Stadium, Heinz Field is a venue that takes special note when the home team enters the Red Zone (at or inside the opponents' 20-yard line). And red is definitely the operative word here. Not blood red, thankfully, but ketchup red.

When the Steelers reach or cross their foes' 20-yard line, two giant Heinz ketchup bottles tilt and appear to fill the scoreboard up with ketchup. I'll take that over a loud volley from a pirate ship any day.

Of the eight games I've seen here, three really stand out, all of which I attended with my friend Dave Brown, a fellow *North County Times* alum and the coolest Steelers fan you'll ever meet. Often, this hobby of mine has enabled me to maintain contact with friends who've moved far away from San Diego. In Dave's case, it actually helped forge our friendship. We knew each other at the newspaper, but not very well when he headed back East in the late 1990s.

It wasn't until 2003, when I tried to find someone to join me for an Eagles game in their new stadium that a mutual friend told me Dave lived near Philly and might be interested in going to the game. Since then we've become good friends with a mutual admiration for not only NFL football, but classic TV shows of the 1960s and 1970s.

Now, about those three games I mentioned ...

Browns-Steelers 2005: Steelers QB Ben Roethlisberger was out with a knee injury, so backup QB Charlie Batch started for Pittsburgh. He suffered a broken hand in the first half, though, and third-stringer Tommy Maddox quarterbacked the team the rest of the way. Even so, it was a wide receiver, Antwaan Randle El, who made the throw of the game, a 51-yard TD strike to wide receiver Hines Ward as the Steelers beat the Browns 34-21.

It would turn out to be a preview of what would happen in Super Bowl XL nearly three months later. In that game, Randle El connected again with Ward for a TD, this time from 43 yards, for the final score in the Steelers' fifth Super Bowl win, 21-10 over the Seattle Seahawks.

Ravens-Steelers 2008: For this rivalry game, the Steelers wore not only throwback jerseys, but throwback yellow helmets, too. As for the game itself, Pittsburgh won in overtime 23-20 on a 46-yard field goal by Steelers kicker Jeff Reed. As much as I enjoyed the ending of this game, I had no idea my stay at Heinz Field was only at the halfway point. I ended up waiting almost four hours for a cab to take me back to my hotel.

This was definitely an outlier for me, as my experiences with cabs and NFL games have generally been very good. But if you're looking for a unique way to get to Heinz Field, take one of the ferry boats there. It's a nice ride, and short, too.

Chargers-Steelers 2008: My only snow game, it came down pretty good early in the first quarter and then stopped, but it stayed chilly. The Chargers scored in the first quarter on a 3-yard run by LaDainian Tomlinson, and later stopped the Steelers on fourth and goal at the 1. As well as the defense played, though, the Chargers' offense could only muster 10 points, and the Steelers finally took the lead at 11-10 by virtue of a field goal with five seconds left. Then came the play that will be talked about in Las Vegas for years.

The Chargers tried to lateral in desperation on the final play of the game, but one of the backward passes was pulled in by Steelers safety Troy Polamalu. He ended up scoring a touchdown, but the officials ruled, incorrectly as the crew chief later admitted, that one of the Chargers' laterals was a forward one, thereby negating the touchdown and leaving the score at 11-10, the first game in league history to end in that exact score. For what it's worth, I thought it was a touchdown, too.

Since the score stayed the same, that meant the Steelers failed to cover the point spread, costing bettors $32 million, according to press reports. Who'd think the number 11 could turn out to be so unlucky in Las Vegas?

CHAPTER THIRTY-SIX
FLY, EAGLES FLY!

Lincoln Financial Field	Philadelphia, PA
Games Seen There: 9	First Game: Oct. 5, 2003
	Last Game: Oct. 6, 2019

My first game here also happened to be the Eagles' first regular-season win in their new home. Speaking of which, I really have to compliment the builders of new and renovated stadiums used by NFL teams in the past 20-plus years, especially when it comes to accessible seating. By placing disabled seating on platforms, gone are the days when I would have to stand most of a game, even though it was sometimes painful to do so, just so I could see what was happening on the field in front of me. I'm glad I no longer have to stand to see NFL action, and I'm especially happy for those for whom standing is not an option.

Special thanks to a friend of mine from high school, Mary Remington Meakim, who always lends me a hand when I come out for Eagles games in Philly, either joining me for them when circumstances permit or just picking me up from the airport, taking me out to dinner and then to my hotel.

Three games of the nine I've seen here stand out, plus one honorable mention.

Washington-Eagles 2003: My first game here, which I attended with my friend Dave Brown, a die-hard Steelers fan who actually lives just outside Philadelphia. This is one of my favorite NFL stadiums. The views are great and so is the atmosphere, especially when fans are singing the team's fight song, "Fly, Eagles Fly." Twice Philadelphia held at least a 10-point lead, only to see Washington claw back to tie or keep the game close. In the last minute of the game, Washington QB Patrick Ramsey was unable to connect on a two-point conversion pass to Laveranues Coles, and the Eagles held on for the 27-25 victory.

Cowboys-Eagles 2005: Eagles fans are probably still kicking themselves over this game slipping away, especially to their hated Cowboys. Philadelphia had the ball and a 20-14 lead with less than three minutes left in the game. On second down and 7 yards to go, Eagles QB Donovan McNabb threw a pass that was intercepted by Cowboys safety Roy Williams and returned for a touchdown. After Cowboys kicker Shaun Suisham made the extra point, Dallas led 21-20. Even worse, McNabb was hurt trying to tackle Williams and was ineffective on the Eagles' next series of downs.

Philadelphia did get one more chance to win the game, following a punt and 23-yard return by Brian Westbrook, the Eagles had the ball on their 35-yard line with 45 seconds left and no timeouts. Kudos to backup QB Mike McMahon, who came in the game in place of McNabb and drove the team down to the Cowboys' 42-yard line. With four seconds left, Eagles kicker David Akers tried a 60-yard field goal to win the game. I remember rooting very hard for Akers to make this kick, even more so when I heard Eagles radio play-by-play announcer Merrill Reese say he and color commentator Mike Quick would jump out of the booth if Akers' kick was good. Unfortunately it was not, as that would have been quite a sight!

Chargers-Eagles 2013: Of all the Chargers games I attended when I was a die-hard fan of that franchise, this ranks near the top of the list. Not only was it a road win, but I attended it with former *North County Times* colleague Jaime Bowden, who has joined me for several games back East, from Cleveland to Charlotte. Throw in that it was against new Eagles head coach Chip Kelly's fast-paced offense, and it was fun seeing the Chargers match Michael Vick and Co.

score for score. Bolts kicker Nick Novak broke a 30-all tie with four seconds left to win the game 33-30.

Honorable mention, Vikings-Eagles 2016: What made this game special was that I went to it not only with Dave and Mary but also another wonderful person from high school whom I hadn't seen or even talked to since the day we graduated: Jacqueline Haut Evans. Getting reacquainted with Jackie and spending another game day with Dave and Mary made for a thoroughly enjoyable afternoon. I just wish it hadn't been so windy. We had to contend with wind gusts of 20-plus mph all day long!

Post-500 commentary: Now that Jaime works as an English teacher, when I decided to purchase tickets to the Jets-Eagles game in 2019, I couldn't resist asking her if she would like to join me for the world's loudest spelling bee. It seemed an apt description, given how fans of those franchises love to yell-spell their team's name.

Alas, it was a one-sided competition. The Eagles dominated this game so thoroughly, winning 31-6, that I don't think I heard a single J-E-T-S! JETS! JETS! JETS! cheer the whole day.

Lastly, a moment of remembrance for a special friend who loved the Eagles almost as much as life itself. Mike Mansur, who passed away in 2020 at the much-too-young age of 52, was as dedicated a football fan as I've ever known. I'm forever grateful that the Eagles won a Super Bowl title before he left this world. Rest in peace, Mike. From now on, whenever I see the Eagles play, I'll think of you and smile, knowing that you're still rooting for them.

CHAPTER THIRTY-SEVEN
A BIG, BEAUTIFUL STADIUM OUT IN THE MIDDLE OF NOWHERE

FedEx Field	Landover, MD
Games Seen There: 7	First Game: Dec. 7, 1998
	Last Game: Oct. 24, 2017

When I say big, I mean BIG! I've witnessed only three games where the attendance was at least 80,000 people, and all three took place here. The largest crowd was 90,487, for a Washington-Cleveland game in 2008 that I attended with former *North County Times* colleague Morgan Loosli, who'd relocated to Washington, D.C. Unfortunately, there's not much around the stadium, which I believe hurts its ambiance. As for exactly where it is, that was an issue, too, for a while.

When this place first opened, it was known as Jack Kent Cooke Stadium, in honor of the franchise's longtime owner who financed its construction. Newspaper datelines from games said they took place in Raljon, Maryland. It turns out that was a legal alternative address Cooke registered with the Postal Service as a tribute to his sons, Ralph and John. Once Daniel Snyder bought the club, that was dropped, and the actual city where the stadium resides, Landover, Maryland, was recognized in datelines.

I've seen three unforgettable games here and one that was forgettable for everyone but me, ex-NCT colleague Dave Brown, who joined me for it, the Philadelphia Eagles and their fans.

San Diego-Washington 1998: When I saw my first game at this stadium, I could be forgiven for believing in some respects that it was a home game for the Chargers. Not only did the team wear its navy blue home jerseys, the weather that day was in the 70s, quite unusual for Maryland in December. In fact, it was actually a few degrees warmer here that day than it was in San Diego.

As for the game itself, it was a seesaw affair, with the Chargers taking a 20-17 lead midway through the fourth quarter on a John Carney field goal. Unfortunately, the Bolts couldn't run down the clock when given the chance with about three minutes left. Trent Green then led Washington 44 yards for the winning score, the final 20 yards coming on a TD pass to Leslie Shepherd, who was so wide open it looked as though he had his own ZIP code.

Indianapolis-Washington 2002: This was the second game of my first NFL doubleheader, the first game having taken place in Baltimore a few hours earlier. Special thanks to my friend Giovanni Prestigiacomo who joined me for both games. I've done two NFL doubleheaders since then, both times combining games in Cleveland and Pittsburgh, but this one is the one I cherish the most. Not only was it the first time I accomplished this feat, it was a lot easier to do, with only 32 miles separating the two NFL stadiums in Maryland, while there's more than 100 miles separating the ones in Cleveland and Pittsburgh.

As for the game, it matched up Washington coach Steve Spurrier against Colts quarterback Peyton Manning. Spurrier didn't have much luck as an NFL head coach, going only 12-20 in his two seasons with Washington. But even during a rocky tenure in the NFL, he still got the better of Manning, as he did as head coach of the University of Florida when facing the University of Tennessee during Peyton's days there. Despite Manning throwing two fourth-quarter touchdown passes that night, Spurrier's squad prevailed, 26-21.

New Orleans-Washington 2015: This game was a 47-14 blowout win for Washington, but it still contained a memorable moment thanks to singer Lee Greenwood, famous for his patriotic anthem "God Bless the USA." After singing his signature tune, Greenwood was invited up to the radio broadcast booth and given the chance to broadcast a play for the home team. I was listening to the broadcast on my headphones while watching the game, as I usually do.

After announcing one play, a two-yard gain by running back Matt Jones, Greenwood was playfully teased by the team's announcers about the poor result of the play, and he asked to do one more. They acquiesced, and on the next play Jones took a screen pass 78 yards for a touchdown.

The announcers congratulated Greenwood on his call, though as the *Washington Post* noted about Greenwood's appearance in the booth, he initially called the score a goal, then corrected himself and said touchdown. I'll defer to the *Post* on exactly what Greenwood said after calling the score. Apparently he said "I told you, give me one more down, that's all I need."

The forgettable game? The one where Donovan McNabb started for Washington against his former Philadelphia squad just hours after signing a huge contract extension. On the first play from scrimmage, Eagles QB Michael Vick completed an 88-yard TD pass to DeSean Jackson. It was 28-0 Philadelphia at the end of the first quarter and 35-0 before Washington finally got on the scoreboard. The final score? Philadelphia 59 Washington 28.

Dave and I had no strong rooting interest in the game, but its conclusion gave us a great sense of satisfaction. In under 48 hours we had seen three NFL games, something I'll bet very few NFL fans have done. We started in Cleveland, where the Jets topped the Browns on a 37-yard TD pass with just 16 seconds left in overtime to win 26-20, then drove to Pittsburgh and saw the Steelers lose to the Patriots 39-26, followed by the runaway win by the Eagles the next night in Maryland.

CHAPTER THIRTY-EIGHT
A KC MASTERPIECE

Arrowhead Stadium	Kansas City, MO
Games Seen There: 13	First Game: Sept. 20, 1998
	Last Game: Nov. 26, 2017

When I first visited Arrowhead in 1998, I could not believe how red most of the seats were and how LOUD the place could get. That took some getting used to. As I visited more often I got to partake in a tradition almost as important as the game itself: tailgating. When it comes to that sport, Arrowhead is right up there with anyone.

And no one throws a better tailgate party at Arrowhead than the Hodes family. Run by Jesse Hodes, the gathering is a perfect mix of good food, drinks and camaraderie, as everyone gets primed for the game. Special thanks to my former *North County Times* colleague (and die-hard Chiefs fan) Monica Hodes-Smail, who invited me to these gatherings.

Chargers-Chiefs 1998: We'll have to start at the beginning, my first game here. That one was so awful from the Chargers' perspective, only Natrone Means' explosive 72-yard romp for a touchdown in the third quarter kept this from being a total disaster. Chargers rookie QB Ryan Leaf completed just 1 of 15 passes for four yards with two interceptions. The headline in the Kansas City Star sports section from the following day sadly summed up Leaf's performance: "Ryan's Hopeless."

Jets-Chiefs 1998: This was one of the most impulsive moves I ever made while pursuing 500 games. Right after the Chargers-Chiefs game in September, I went to the Chiefs ticket office and bought a ticket for this Nov. 1 game. I was unable to get the previous day off from work or a same-day flight out of San Diego in time for kickoff, so my friend Kurt Rowland drove me up to Los Angeles at 4 a.m. so I could catch a 7 a.m. nonstop flight to Kansas City the day of the game. Everything went just right, and I made it to the game on time — but just barely. The game itself was worth all the hassle, going right down to the wire. The Jets prevailed 20-17 when kicker John Hall made a 32-yard field goal with no time left on the clock.

I'm happy it all worked out, but since then I've vowed never again to be on such a razor's edge when it comes to making it to a game on time, especially one so far away.

Chargers-Chiefs 2010: This was the second part of the only MLB-NFL doubleheader I've ever done. I saw the Oakland A's play the Kansas City Royals at 2 p.m. in beautiful sunny weather, then went across the Kauffman Stadium parking lot for a "Monday Night Football" game that kicked off at 9:20 p.m. local time. By then, the weather had changed considerably and become rainy and very windy. The Bolts pulled within seven points of the Chiefs in the third quarter but could get no closer. Wide receiver Malcom Floyd could not pull in QB Philip Rivers' fourth-down pass with 33 seconds left in the game. I had been fortunate to be able to watch the game under cover but after it ended, my luck ran out as well. I got completely soaked in the stadium parking lot waiting for a ride back to my hotel. The shuttle I had taken from there had already made its final run. Luckily for me, two Chiefs employees were kind enough to help me get back there.

Patriots-Chiefs 2014: In the 21st century the Patriots have been in nine Super Bowls. They appeared in five from 2002 to 2012, winning three, and four more from 2015 to 2019, again winning three. If ever there was a dividing line between those two eras, I'd say it's the 41-14 shellacking they took from the Chiefs this night. Almost immediately, media began writing about the imminent demise of the Patriots' dynasty, while in reality it was merely about to enter a new phase.

Brady did not have a good game, throwing for only 159 yards

and two interceptions, the second of which, his last pass of the night, was returned for a touchdown by Kansas City. New England's last touchdown came via a 13-yard pass from Jimmy Garoppolo to tight end Rob Gronkowski. After the game, Patriots coach Bill Belichick just kept issuing his now-legendary mantra. "We're on to Cincinnati." Looks like he knew what he was talking about.

This was also the game where the Chiefs set the record for loudest stadium at 142.4 decibels. Thank God I had ear plugs handy to endure the din.

Rams-Chiefs 2014: This was not a close game at all, as the Rams lost 34-7 to their then in-state rivals, though they did briefly hold the lead at 7-0. It deserves honorable mention because of who joined me for it, another former NCT colleague, Erin Shetler, who was attending her first NFL game, her cousin Andy, and the circumstances surrounding it. Erin left the NCT for the *St. Louis Post Dispatch*. She knew of my cross-country hobby and said she'd love to join me for a Rams game in Missouri, back when they called the Gateway City home.

In 2014, Erin did just that, although she did have to go west 250 miles to Kansas City for a Rams game with me, given my requirement for a grass field, something that wasn't part of the Edward Jones Dome's business plan. Luckily for me, she didn't take the lopsided loss personally. Even better was the fact that Erin has family in Kansas City, so it made for a fun road trip no matter how the game turned out.

Broncos-Chiefs 2014: Never have I been more bundled up for a game than this one. I wore a fleece mask for the first time in my life. The kickoff temperature was 27 degrees, and the wind chill was in single digits by the fourth quarter. My eternal thanks to friends Beth and Mike Boucher, who joined me for this game. I might not have survived it without them. They provided the fleece mask.

As cold as we were, that's how hot the Broncos were that night. Though his physical skills were diminishing, Peyton Manning still was able to complete the passes he had to for Denver to win going away, 29-16.

Broncos-Chiefs 2017: I'm back in Arrowhead for another prime-time game between these AFC West rivals. Thankfully it's about 20 degrees warmer on this night. And not only that, it's a special occasion, Game 499 (and my 50th Chiefs game, too).

The Chiefs were kind enough to let me and the two people who joined me for the game that night, Monica's brother Eric and his beautiful wife, Eliza, watch pregame warmups down on the sidelines. I even got to briefly chat with Chiefs owner Clark Hunt and Tammi Reid, wife of the team's head coach, Andy Reid. Both said they were impressed that I'd seen so many NFL games in person. I thanked them for their kind words and told them how pleased I was that Game 499 was taking place in Kansas City, given all that the Hunt family has done for pro football.

Post-500 commentary: Not long after Game 499 here, I was back at Arrowhead less than a month later to fulfill a promise I made to Monica many years ago, that one day we would see a game here together. Not only did I attend the game with Monica, her sister Emily Hodes Gratzinger, joined us as well.

We had a great time even though the Chiefs ended up losing to the Bills. That day, I was wearing a Chiefs jersey gifted to me by the Hodes family in October at one of their tailgate parties. I was asked to name my favorite Chiefs player. Shortly after I said Alex Smith, in part because he grew up in San Diego just like me, I was given a replica jersey of his, which I wore with pride at Arrowhead that fall.

I had no idea it would soon become an antique only months later by the emergence of one of the greatest players to come along in a generation, the incomparable Patrick Mahomes.

CHAPTER THIRTY-NINE
NO BETTER PLACE TO BE
FOR AN NFL GAME

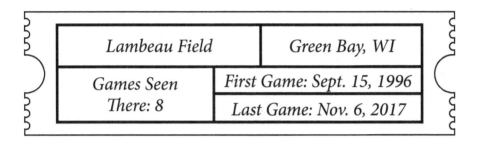

Lambeau Field	Green Bay, WI
Games Seen There: 8	First Game: Sept. 15, 1996
	Last Game: Nov. 6, 2017

In some ways this place was the Alpha as well as the Omega of my football odyssey. My first trip to Green Bay in 1996 to see the Chargers play the Packers really stirred my imagination about seeing NFL games in faraway places. And it wasn't only the game, just my 30th overall, but also my visit to the Green Bay Packers Hall of Fame & Museum the day before, which gave me an appreciation of just how important the Packers and their current stadium have meant to the NFL. This is why I wanted my 500th NFL game to be at Lambeau Field.

Since that game, that legend has grown exponentially, with numerous unforgettable moments added by Brett Favre, Reggie White and Aaron Rodgers, among others, and two Lombardi trophies to join the two Super Bowl titles won in the Lombardi era itself.

That turned out to be the first Super Bowl-winning season for the Packers in almost 30 years. Though I was still a die-hard Dolphins fan at the time, even wearing a Dolphins sweatshirt to the game, I was hoping the Chargers would win. Unfortunately for the Bolts, the Packers were unstoppable that day. Brett Favre threw three TD passes while Reggie White had two sacks. LeRoy Butler and Desmond Howard put exclamation points on the victory in the fourth quarter, Butler with a 90-yard interception return, and Howard with a 65-yard punt return. Both ended with the traditional Lambeau Leap.

Near the end of the game, a Chargers fan near me had endured enough of the "GO PACK GO!" cheer and improvised her own cheer: "RUM AND COKE!" Not surprisingly, some of the Bolts fans around me picked it up. I didn't, though. I saw the humor in it, for sure. But I was too impressed by the Packers' play that day to alter their fans' cheer.

Every so often, people publish lists of unforgettable places and events people should try to see if they're fans of a certain sport. If your No. 1 sport is NFL football, this is the one place you must try to see a game, even if you're not a fan of the Packers.

Here are a few more unforgettable games for me at Lambeau.

Falcons-Packers 2002: It certainly wasn't frozen tundra when the mercury reached 88 degrees that day, reportedly the warmest opening-day temperature ever at Lambeau Field. Luckily for those of us who were there, it was also a very entertaining game to help take our minds off the heat. The two teams each scored 34 points in regulation, then the Packers won it with a 34-yard field goal by Ryan Longwell. The Falcons would get their revenge four months later, shocking the Packers by handing them their first playoff loss at Lambeau Field, 27-7. The reported wind chill that day was 30 degrees.

Dolphins-Packers 2002: Speaking of wind chills, it was a couple of degrees colder, 28, at my next game in Lambeau nearly two months later. The game wasn't much, as the Packers easily handled the Dolphins that Monday night, taking a 24-0 lead into the fourth quarter until the Dolphins scored 10 points in the final 8:20 to make the score look more respectable.

At the end of the game, my feet felt like two solid blocks of ice! Still, I couldn't help but feel a sense of pride that I had survived a game at Lambeau where the temperature had gone below freezing. Kind of like the slogan on the old Croix de Candlestick badge the San Francisco

Giants used to hand out to die-hard fans at blustery night games at that venue. The inscription in Latin read: I came, I saw, I survived.

What really made this trip interesting for me was that I had to work the next night in Escondido, California, (2,146 miles away) at the *North County Times* on election night. I made it through OK, though at times I felt like a zombie. Thank God for election night pizza for helping me make it through my shift. And kudos as well to my friend Kurt Rowland, who graciously drove me to and from work that day. I knew I was in no condition to do so.

Browns-Packers 2005: This game itself was highly entertaining, with the Browns shocking the Packers, 26-24, thanks to Trent Dilfer's three TD passes, two of which went for more than 60 yards. The real excitement, though, took place after the game: My wheelchair went missing and then was returned to me, all within a span of five hours.

Here's what happened. After the game, which I attended with Robert Delaval, who I had met during our days at San Diego State University but was then living in Milwaukee, we went back to his truck in the stadium parking lot. We were both tired, and Robert was decidedly irked upon learning the Chargers had just lost a game in the last few seconds that day in Denver, so we waited a while for the traffic to thin out a bit. Robert and I both thought he had already put my wheelchair in his truck and so he drove off.

We learned otherwise when we got back to our hotel. I called the Packers while Robert went back to Lambeau to look for the wheelchair. The Packers said no wheelchair had been turned in and Robert didn't spot it during his search. He did, though, find Ron Schauer, a Green Bay resident, near where we had parked who said he saw two men take an unattended wheelchair and use it to transport a man who apparently was too inebriated to walk. Mr. Schauer told my friend which direction he saw those men go.

After Robert got back to the hotel, I called the Green Bay Police Department and they sent over Officer Mike Knetzger to take a statement from me and Robert, including information provided by Mr. Schauer, about the wheelchair's disappearance. I explained the situation to him, adding that while the wheelchair is nothing special in its own right (it's old and nowhere near as fashionable as today's wheelchairs), I greatly desired its return because of its sentimental value. I got it from a friend in 1984 and have used it for most of the NFL games I've attended.

Within an hour of Officer Knetzger taking my statement, he had found the wheelchair, abandoned in a parking lot not too far from the stadium, and returned it to me at the hotel. I was absolutely ecstatic at its quick return. I've kept a very close eye on it ever since. It did go missing briefly after Game 497 in Philadelphia but United Airlines tracked it down and got it back to me before my next game.

Lions-Packers 2017: "Game 500!" The finish line. I felt so serene, especially once I got to Lambeau Field that night, as though I had just reached the top of Mount Everest.

It wasn't a sherpa who helped me get there, though, but a Hall of Fame wide receiver. James Lofton to be exact.

A couple of years earlier, Fox5 TV in San Diego, did a story about my NFL games hobby. I mentioned then how I hoped to see game 500 at Lambeau Field. James, who often provides commentary on NFL-related stories for the station, saw the story and pledged to help me get tickets for my milestone game.

True to his word, he provided me with access to purchase four tickets for the game. Thank you, James!

And thank you, John Lingham! A friend of mine from high school, John helped bankroll my trip to Titletown for the game when I found myself short of funds that summer. That's par for the course for John, who's involved in several philanthropic endeavors.

Their assistance enabled me to be there with former *North County Times* colleagues Michael Donnelly, who had moved to Madison,

Wisconsin; Cathy Hendrie, a native of Appleton, Wisconsin, and a die-hard Packers fan; and Cathy's partner Jon Norton. Just as I was reaching my goal, I was reminded how much this quest has been about sharing fun experiences with family and friends whenever possible, not just attending football games.

Before we went into Lambeau Field that night, the three of them presented me with a huge chocolate cake in the shape of a football, with frosting that spelled out the occasion. They placed candles on it and lit them, which I promptly blew out. We waited until after we got back to my hotel to have any of the cake, though, so as not to jinx things.

Told in advance what the game meant for me, Packers officials couldn't have been nicer to us, as we were all given pregame field passes. While I was down there, ESPN ran its story about my football journey, then showed me live on the field, unbeknownst to me. Fortunately I didn't do anything embarrassing while the camera was on me.

As for the game itself, it was a bit of a disappointment only because Green Bay QB Aaron Rodgers was unable to play due to injury, and the Packers weren't playing the Bears, my desired foe for this game. The Lions, though, were the perfect substitute. A few years prior, I had set an additional goal of seeing every NFL team play in person 10 times. After game 499, there was only one team left I had yet to see 10 times. As luck would have it, my 500th game, Detroit vs. Green Bay, would also be my 10th Lions game.

All in all, it was a memorable night, a few degrees above freezing and featuring the unique ambiance that is Lambeau Field. True, the Packers lost 30-17, but we still had a wonderful time. Thank you God, family and friends for making this special dream of mine come true.

Post-500 commentary: I don't have immediate plans to return to Lambeau Field, but I certainly would like to come back here for more NFL games, especially the renewal of the NFL's most storied rivalry, Bears-Packers.

CHAPTER FORTY
BEYOND 500

Lots of people asked me what I would do next after seeing game No. 500. What else? No. 501. There's only one proper place to do that. I even made sure to wear a pair of 501 jeans to Levi's Stadium that day.

After that, my next goal became much more localized. With the Chargers and Rams preparing to move into a new stadium in Inglewood, California, with an artificial surface, I decided to attend 200 NFL games in Southern California before that option was gone.

At the start of the 2018 NFL season I had seen 191 NFL games in the region. I became a Rams season-ticket holder, not just to pursue this goal, but also because I decided after the Chargers moved to the L.A. area in 2017, that the Rams and Chiefs would be my new co-favorite teams. I picked the Rams in part because I was deeply hurt by the Chargers' decision to leave San Diego after 56 years of steadfast loyalty by the fan base there, of which I was a proud member for 17 seasons. I also liked that the Rams were going to be playing their home games, at least for a few seasons, in the historic Los Angeles Memorial Coliseum.

The reason for my Chiefs fandom? Lamar Hunt. Every person who is a fan of modern pro football owes an incalculable debt to that man. Without his actions in creating and guiding the American Football League, 10 NFL teams today would never have existed. Nor would the Super Bowl, by that name, anyway.

Speaking of pro football history, several months after seeing my 500th game, I offered the Pro Football Hall of Fame in Canton, Ohio, the memorabilia I accumulated seeing all these NFL games (tickets, programs, photos, next-day sports sections, etc.). The Hall of Fame asked if I would be willing to donate my ticket collection, which I did in person Nov. 3, 2018, the day before I saw my 518th game in Cleveland.

As for the Chiefs and Rams, I was thrilled when I realized these two teams would play each other in the 2018 regular season, even more so when I realized the game would be played at the L.A. Coliseum. I did feel bad, though, for the fans in Mexico City, who lost out on the game when it was moved because of unplayable field conditions.

At halftime, the score was tied at 23. But things were just getting started. There were plenty of offensive fireworks to be sure, but there were also three defensive scores during the game. I dubbed it "The Track Meet" in a nod to the L.A. Coliseum's Olympic track and field history. Final score: Rams 54, Chiefs 51. The first time in NFL history a team had scored at least 50 points and lost.

I had witnessed one of the greatest football games ever played. In fact, the only game I would rank above it that I've seen live would be Super Bowl XLIX.

The Rams' second-round playoff game against the Dallas Cowboys gave me my 200th NFL game in SoCal, so I sought another goal.

I discovered it quite by accident. I was looking at the list of games I was thinking of seeing next season and comparing it to my list of NFL teams and how many times I'd seen each one play in person. I noticed many were just over 20, and then it hit me. Twenty-five would be the ideal number. It's exactly 100 quarters of game action, a mark I expect to reach with 12 teams by the conclusion of the 2021 NFL season.

And unlike my 500 games quest, where every game could only count once toward that goal, seeing a game where both teams were under the 25-game mark would count twice. If things go as planned, I'll reach 25 games with both the Bears and the Steelers when I see them play each other on Monday, Nov. 8, 2021.

I estimate it will take me about 10-15 more years before I will have seen every NFL team play that many times in person. Wish me luck!

CHAPTER FORTY-ONE
"RAIDERS DRAW FULL HOUSE FOR OPENER"

Allegiant Stadium	Las Vegas, NV
Games Seen There: 2	First Game: Sept. 13, 2021
	Last Game: Oct. 10, 2021

This game between the Ravens and Raiders, the first one in Las Vegas that fans could attend, and the first in person for me in nearly 20 months, was not only very entertaining, it also gave me a new state and stadium where I've witnessed NFL action in person.

I've now attended NFL games in 18 different states and 36 different venues. The last time I added a new state and structure at the same time was back in 2005, when I saw the Buccaneers play the Saints at LSU Tiger Stadium in Baton Rouge, Louisiana.

While I appreciate that the Raiders' move to Las Vegas has given me the chance to experience another state-of-the-art sports palace, my heart when it comes to Raiders football will always be in Oakland. If Tony Bennett can leave his on the other side of the Bay Bridge, I can leave mine there. The best Raiders shirt I saw this Monday night read: "What happens in Vegas ... started in Oakland."

The Raiders actually called Kezar Stadium and Candlestick Park in San Francisco home when they began play in 1960. But I digress.

Allegiant Stadium is an impressive-looking facility and had a full house that night, 65,000 people not only ready for some football, but happy to escape the 100-plus-degree desert heat outside. Even indoors, you could easily be reminded of it. The sun is plainly visible on the skin of the roof covering.

As warm as the sun was outdoors, that's how green the grass was indoors. It reminded me of the Arizona Cardinals' home field at State Farm Stadium in Glendale, Arizona. No surprise there; the Raiders solicited advice from the Cardinals on how to maintain the top-flight grass surface that Raiders owner Mark Davis insisted on when moving his team to Las Vegas.

My friend Robert Delaval and I had a little trouble navigating the elevators here, but other than that it's easy to get around once you're inside the place. Some features in the seating area that really caught my attention were the team's house band stationed near one of the end zones, a Break Time Remaining Clock that showed how much time was left in a TV timeout and three large video boards.

I was very glad Robert was able to join me for my inaugural game here. He made the roughly six-hour drive from San Diego, all while graciously putting up with my preference for 1970s soft-rock music on XM radio. We've now seen NFL games in eight different stadiums, second only to my friend Jeff Darby, who's been with me for NFL action in 11 different venues.

Having the Empress of Soul herself, Gladys Knight, perform the national anthem added to the luster of this prime-time event.

A personal highlight of the evening for me was meeting up with fellow *North County Times* alum Holly Lobelson Silvestri, who I hadn't seen in more than 20 years, and her husband, Rob, at halftime.

As for the game itself, it was an exciting, seesaw affair that the Raiders were able to tie late and then eventually win in overtime. In true Las Vegas style, two long shots (a 55-yard field goal and a 31-yard touchdown pass) came in for the Raiders. Helping set up the winning play for the Raiders was defensive end Carl Nassib, the first publicly gay active NFL player. He sacked Ravens QB Lamar Jackson, forcing a fumble which was recovered by fellow defensive end Darius Philon. Two plays later, Raiders QB Derek Carr connected with wide receiver Zay Jones for the winning score.

My next Raiders game in Las Vegas, on Oct. 10 vs. the Chicago Bears, proved to be just as memorable on a personal level. It was my girlfriend Danelle Palm's first NFL game!

CHAPTER FORTY-TWO
LEGACY

My journey in pursuit of attending 500 NFL games has been well documented over the years in newspaper articles and stories on TV. And I've enjoyed reliving this odyssey by writing this book.

As pleased as I am to have reached this goal, and hopeful of attaining my next one of seeing every NFL team play in person 25 times, they both pale in comparison to the sense of pride and satisfaction I have in knowing that for 20-plus years, I was a working journalist.

Seeing football games is my hobby. Copy editing was my profession. If I've left any legacy in my life, it will be because of the work I did in the newspaper industry, with people I feel privileged to call friends and colleagues, not for seeing a lot of football games.

Hall of Famer James Lofton heard about my goal and made it possible for me to buy four tickets to my 500th NFL game at Lambeau Field in 2017. This is a picture of me and Lofton a few months before the game.

This is a picture of me at Lambeau Field before my 500th NFL game.

I donated all my game tickets I had saved on my quest to attend 500 games to the Pro Football Hall of Fame in November 2018. This is a photo of me and my ticket to the 500th game, as I handed it over to Hall of Fame archivist Jon Kendle.

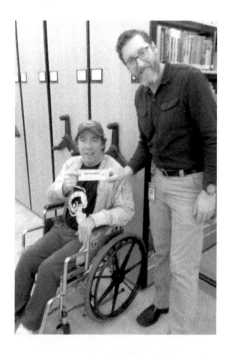

That's me with two fingers up on the day I saw my 200th game, Bills vs. Chargers, on Nov. 20, 2005. The Chargers won, 48-10.

Game No. 300 in November 2009, in Charlotte, North Carolina. Sadly, that grass field was replaced by FieldTurf in 2021.

Four fingers up for 400 games, this time in Arizona in 2013.

My friend and former co-worker Cathy Hendrie has joined me for several games over the years, including Game 170, Packers-Chargers, on Dec. 14, 2003. If her hat doesn't give it away, she's a die-hard Packers fan. I'll always remember this game because Saddam Hussein's capture dominated the news that day.

Kent Davy, the former editor of the North County Times, where I worked for much of my newspaper career, joined me for Game 468, Broncos-Chargers at San Diego's Qualcomm Stadium.

The smile was frozen on my face after Game 144, Dolphins-Packers, in Green Bay in November 2002. The temperature at the start of the game was 30 degrees, wind chill 28. It felt much colder three hours later.

Friends Michael Donnelly, Jon Norton and Cathy Hendrie join me in acknowledging my milestone game at Lambeau Field on Nov. 6, 2017.

My friends, Chicago natives Jill Laramie and Jan Gonzalez (yes, they're twins), joined me for Game 492, Vikings-Bears in October 2017. Their brother Jay Latasiewicz was one of my bus drivers when I attended San Diego State University, and the entire Latasiewicz family has helped me to see many football and baseball games in Chicago.

I like to listen to the broadcast of a game while I watch it.

This is the only time I've been at a snowy game, and it's the only time in NFL history that the final score ended up 11-10. The Steelers beat the Chargers in Game 271 in November 2008.

My friend Tom Graves met me for Game 477, Dolphins-Rams, in November 2016. It was Tom's first NFL game ever and my first at the L.A. Memorial Coliseum since 1993.

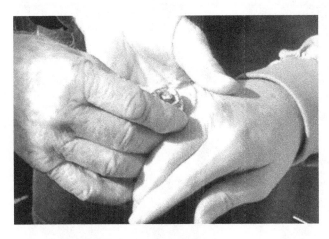

When Bob Griese
was a member of
the Dolphins' radio
crew, two friends
of mine, Jay Paris
and Bryce Miller,
secretly arranged for
me to meet him. My
friends let the dolphin
out of the bag and
back in the water
pretty quickly, but it
was still a thrill for
him to show up at
Jay's tailgate party
before Game 458 in
December 2015 and
sign the Griese jersey
I bought the day he
was inducted into the
Hall of Fame in 1990.
It was extra special for
him to let me briefly
wear his Super Bowl
VII ring from 1973,
when the Dolphins
completed their
perfect season. I was
7 years old then, and
I've never forgotten
that game.

My friend Lauri
Lockwood, a former
co-worker of mine,
joined me for a few
Chargers games in
San Diego. Here
we are at Packers-
Chargers, Game 77, in
October 1999.

Nahshon Menefee and Jeanelle Cabello joined me at Game 488, Cowboys-Cardinals in September 2017, in Glendale, Ariz. Jeanelle worked at a hotel where I stayed once for another Cardinals game, and when I told her I needed a ride to the game, she asked Nahshon to help me. Since then, we've attended at least one game a year together.

Two fingers for another NFL double-header, Nov. 14, 2010, a day with my friend Dave Brown that started in Cleveland for Jets-Browns and ended in Pittsburgh for Patriots-Steelers, Games 327 and 328.

My girlfriend Danelle Palm attended the Bears-Raiders game with me in October 2021. It was my 546th game and Danelle's first.

Thomas Neumann, a former co-worker of mine, joined me for Game 473 in Tampa in November 2016. It was the first time we'd seen each other in more than 20 years.

I was the happiest I've ever been as a Chargers fan here with my friend Sean Bohan. It was right after the Colts-Chargers playoff game in January 2009, Game 282, which the Chargers won in overtime over Peyton Manning and the Colts.

My uncle Bruce Reiman has attended several games with me in Cleveland over the years.

I worked with Dave Brown at the North County Times. He's a die-hard Steelers fan, but he's fine with seeing Eagles games in Philadelphia, too, such as this one, Game 471, in October 2016.

In December 1996, I attended Game 34, Chargers-Bears, my first one at Soldier Field in Chicago. It was one of the first games I saw in this wheelchair, which I still use today when going to games.

My lifelong friend Dawn Siskowic Adams and her husband, Paul Adams, joined me for Game 224, Broncos-Chargers, in December 2006.

This photo was taken at FedEx Field in Landover, Md., after the second game (Colts-Washington) of my first NFL doubleheader, Oct. 27, 2002. My friend Giovanni Prestigiacomo and I started the day in Baltimore for Steelers-Ravens. They were Games 141 and 142.

My friend Erin Shetler said she wanted to join me for a St. Louis Rams game in Missouri. She did, Game 424 in October 2014, but she had to travel to Kansas City to do it.

At this game against the Cowboys in Kansas City in October 2009 (No. 290 for me), the Chiefs celebrated the 50th anniversary of the American Football League.

My friend Tim Reeve was my partner for Game 478 in Oakland in November 2016, when the Raiders beat the Panthers, 35-32.

My friend Cindy Gipson met up with me in December 2018 for Game 522, Broncos-49ers, my 75th San Francisco 49ers game. Cindy and I met on a plane and whenever we know we're both going to be at Levi's Stadium, we make it a point to meet up and say hello.

My friends Amanda Selvidio (left) and Sabrina Prestigiacomo, shortly after the conclusion of the Patriots-Chargers playoff game in January 2007, Game 230. The Patriots prevailed, which is clearly evidenced by Amanda's radiant smile.

Jaime Bowden, a friend and former co-worker, has joined me for several games, including this one in Philadelphia, Game 529. The Eagles won, 31-6.

Two high school friends joined me for Game 471, Vikings-Eagles, in October 2016: Mary Remington Meakim, left, and Jacqueline Haut Evans.

I can always count on Mary Remington Meakim to be at my side in Philadelphia. She joins me at a game there when she can, like this time (Game 497, Washington-Eagles). If she can't go to the game, though, I know she'll meet me for a meal or even be good for a ride from the airport.

There aren't many early photos documenting my love of football, but a few have survived from those Kodak Fotomat days, including these. In the first two, you can see me playing. (The Nerf football is blurry in the first one because my release was so lightning-quick.) The third is the only photographic evidence of me seeing my hero, Miami Dolphins quarterback Bob Griese, play. The picture is from the second NFL game I ever attended, Dolphins-Chargers in October 1978, a gift from my parents for my 13th birthday.

The Dolphins-Jaguars playoff game in January 2000, Game 89, was Dan Marino's final game and my last as a Dolphins fan.

My friend Annette Kennedy, who I worked with at Sun Newspapers in San Diego County, has gone with me to many games over the years, including this one, Game 280, Chargers-Buccaneers in Tampa.

This is me with my niece Keely Engesath's husband, Mykell, at Game 539, the Rams' last game at the Los Angeles Memorial Coliseum in December 2019, before the team moved to Sofi Stadium in Inglewood.

My friend Monica Hodes-Smail joined me at Bills-Chiefs, Game 503, in 2017.

Amanda Selvidio, a fellow former NCT employee, joined me in September 2016 for Game 463, Patriots-Cardinals. It was the third time I had seen the Patriots at what's now known as State Farm Stadium, but it was the first time seeing them play the NFL tenant there, the Cardinals. The other two times were for Super Bowls XLII and XLIX.

Friend and former NCT co-worker Greg Anderson joined me for Game 132, the first regular-season game at Gillette Stadium in September 2002. Greg picked me up from my hotel in Rhode Island, where I was staying because Providence is closer to the stadium than Boston. It's the only time I've ever been to Rhode Island.

This was taken
at Game 205,
Eagles-Cardinals
in December 2005,
the last Cardinals
game at Sun Devil
Stadium.

My friend Robert
Delaval has joined
me for NFL games
at eight different
stadiums, including
this one, Game 488
in September 2017,
in Glendale, Ariz.

This is me after one
of the 71 Raiders
games I saw at the
Oakland-Alameda
County Coliseum.

Former NCT colleagues Melanie and Scott Marshall joined me for Game 455, Broncos-Chargers, on Dec. 6, 2015, the same day Fox5 San Diego did a story on me and my quest to see 500 NFL games played on grass.

This was my first game in Baltimore after the Ravens switched back to a grass field in 2016. It was Game 475, Browns-Ravens in November of that year.

Where fashion meets football: That's me in my 501s at Levi's Stadium in Santa Clara for Game 501. The 49ers played the Giants that day in November 2017.

Monica Hodes-Smail and her husband Eric, joined me for Game 454, Chiefs-Chargers in November 2015, at Qualcomm Stadium.

Jaime Bowden joined me for Game 453, Saints-Washington, in November 2015.

Me with a statue of Don Shula, legendary, two-time Super Bowl-winning head coach of the Miami Dolphins, at what is now called Hard Rock Stadium.

CHAPTER FORTY-THREE
THE LIST

DATE	CITY	STADIUM	SCORE
12-04-77	San Diego	San Diego Stadium	Chargers 37 Browns 14
10-15-78	San Diego	San Diego Stadium	Dolphins 28 Chargers 21
11-18-84	San Diego	SD Jack Murphy Stadium	Chargers 34 Dolphins 28
09-29-85	San Diego	SD Jack Murphy Stadium	Browns 21 Chargers 7
11-10-85	San Diego	SD Jack Murphy Stadium	Chargers 40 Raiders 34
– 5 –			
09-07-86	San Diego	SD Jack Murphy Stadium	Chargers 50 Dolphins 28
09-21-86	San Diego	SD Jack Murphy Stadium	Washington 30 Chargers 27
10-09-88	Los Angeles	L.A. Memorial Coliseum	Dolphins 24 Raiders 14
12-11-88	San Diego	SD Jack Murphy Stadium	Chargers 20 Steelers 14
12-03-89	San Diego	SD Jack Murphy Stadium	Jets 20 Chargers 17
– 10 –			
12-29-90	Tempe	Sun Devil Stadium	Eagles 23 Cardinals 21
11-17-91	San Diego	SD Jack Murphy Stadium	Chargers 24 Saints 21
12-08-91	Tempe	Sun Devil Stadium	Washington 20 Cardinals 14
12-15-91	San Diego	SD Jack Murphy Stadium	Chargers 38 Dolphins 30
11-22-92	San Diego	SD Jack Murphy Stadium	Chargers 29 Buccaneers 14

DATE	CITY	STADIUM	SCORE
– 15 –			
12-06-92	Tempe	Sun Devil Stadium	Chargers 27 Cardinals 21
10-10-93	Cleveland	Cleveland Municipal Stadium	Dolphins 24 Browns 14
10-31-93	Los Angeles	L.A. Memorial Coliseum	Chargers 30 Raiders 23
12-05-93	Tempe	Sun Devil Stadium	Cardinals 38 Rams 10
12-26-93	Anaheim	Anaheim Stadium	Browns 42 Rams 14
– 20 –			
12-27-93	San Diego	SD Jack Murphy Stadium	Chargers 45 Dolphins 20
10-09-94	San Diego	SD Jack Murphy Stadium	Chargers 20 Chiefs 6
11-27-94	San Diego	SD Jack Murphy Stadium	Chargers 31 Rams 17
12-24-94	Anaheim	Anaheim Stadium	Washington 24 Rams 21
09-03-95	Oakland	Oakland-Alameda County Coliseum	Raiders 17 Chargers 7
– 25 –			
11-05-95	San Diego	SD Jack Murphy Stadium	Dolphins 24 Chargers 14
12-10-95	Clemson	Clemson Memorial Stadium	49ers 31 Panthers 10
12-11-95	Miami	Joe Robbie Stadium	Dolphins 13 Chiefs 6
09-08-96	Tempe	Sun Devil Stadium	Dolphins 38 Cardinals 10
09-15-96	Green Bay	Lambeau Field	Packers 42 Chargers 10
– 30 –			
09-29-96	San Diego	SD Jack Murphy Stadium	Chargers 22 Chiefs 19

DATE	CITY	STADIUM	SCORE
11-11-96	San Diego	SD Jack Murphy Stadium	Chargers 27 Lions 21
12-01-96	Oakland	Oakland-Alameda County Coliseum	Raiders 17 Dolphins 7
12-14-96	Chicago	Soldier Field	Bears 27 Chargers 14
08-31-97	Foxboro	Foxboro Stadium	Patriots 41 Chargers 7
– 35 –			
09-14-97	San Diego	Qualcomm Stadium	Panthers 26 Chargers 7
09-21-97	Tampa	Houlihan's Stadium	Buccaneers 31 Dolphins 21
09-28-97	San Diego	Qualcomm Stadium	Chargers 21 Ravens 17
10-05-97	Oakland	Oakland-Alameda County Coliseum	Chargers 25 Raiders 10
10-12-97	Tempe	Sun Devil Stadium	Giants 27 Cardinals 13
– 40 –			
10-19-97	Baltimore	Memorial Stadium	Dolphins 24 Ravens 13
10-26-97	San Diego	Qualcomm Stadium	Chargers 35 Colts 19
11-02-97	Memphis	Liberty Bowl Mem. Stadium	Jaguars 30 Oilers 24
11-09-97	San Diego	Qualcomm Stadium	Seahawks 37 Chargers 31
11-16-97	San Diego	Qualcomm Stadium	Raiders 38 Chargers 13
– 45 –			
11-23-97	San Francisco	3Comm Park	49ers 17 Chargers 10
11-30-97	Oakland	Oakland-Alameda County Coliseum	Dolphins 34 Raiders 16
12-07-97	San Diego	Qualcomm Stadium	Falcons 14 Chargers 3

DATE	CITY	STADIUM	SCORE
12-14-97	San Diego	Qualcomm Stadium	Chiefs 29 Chargers 7
12-21-97	Denver	Mile High Stadium	Broncos 38 Chargers 3
– 50 –			
09-06-98	San Diego	Qualcomm Stadium	Chargers 16 Bills 14
09-13-98	Oakland	Oakland-Alameda County Coliseum	Raiders 20 Giants 17
09-20-98	Kansas City	Arrowhead Stadium	Chiefs 23 Chargers 7
09-27-98	San Diego	Qualcomm Stadium	Giants 34 Chargers 16
10-04-98	Tempe	Sun Devil Stadium	Raiders 23 Cardinals 20
– 55 –			
10-12-98	Jacksonville	Alltel Stadium	Jaguars 28 Dolphins 21
10-18-98	San Diego	Qualcomm Stadium	Chargers 13 Eagles 10
10-25-98	San Diego	Qualcomm Stadium	Seahawks 27 Chargers 20
11-01-98	Kansas City	Arrowhead Stadium	Jets 20 Chiefs 17
11-08-98	Tempe	Sun Devil Stadium	Cardinals 29 Washington 27
– 60 –			
11-15-98	Charlotte	Ericsson Stadium	Dolphins 13 Panthers 9
11-22-98	San Diego	Qualcomm Stadium	Chargers 38 Chiefs 37
11-29-98	San Diego	Qualcomm Stadium	Broncos 31 Chargers 16
12-06-98	Raljon	Jack Kent Cooke Stadium	Washington 24 Chargers 20
12-14-98	San Francisco	3Comm Park	49ers 35 Lions 13

DATE	CITY	STADIUM	SCORE
– 65 –			
12-20-98	San Diego	Qualcomm Stadium	Raiders 17 Chargers 10
12-26-98	Oakland	Oakland-Alameda County Coliseum	Chiefs 31 Raiders 24
12-27-98	Tempe	Sun Devil Stadium	Cardinals 16 Chargers 13
09-12-99	Chicago	Soldier Field	Bears 20 Chiefs 17
09-19-99	Miami	Pro Player Stadium	Dolphins 19 Cardinals 16
– 70 –			
09-26-99	San Diego	Qualcomm Stadium	Colts 27 Chargers 19
09-27-99	Tempe	Sun Devil Stadium	49ers 24 Cardinals 10
10-03-99	San Diego	Qualcomm Stadium	Chargers 21 Chiefs 14
10-10-99	Oakland	Network Assoc. Coliseum	Broncos 16 Raiders 13
10-17-99	San Diego	Qualcomm Stadium	Chargers 13 Seahawks 10
– 75 –			
10-21-99	Baltimore	PSINet Stadium	Chiefs 35 Ravens 8
10-24-99	San Diego	Qualcomm Stadium	Packers 31 Chargers 3
10-31-99	Oakland	Network Assoc. Coliseum	Dolphins 16 Raiders 9
11-07-99	San Diego	Qualcomm Stadium	Broncos 33 Chargers 17
11-14-99	Oakland	Network Assoc. Coliseum	Raiders 28 Chargers 9
– 80 –			
11-21-99	San Diego	Qualcomm Stadium	Bears 23 Chargers 20

DATE	CITY	STADIUM	SCORE
11-28-99	Oakland	Network Assoc. Coliseum	Chiefs 37 Raiders 34
12-05-99	San Diego	Qualcomm Stadium	Chargers 23 Browns 10
12-06-99	Tampa	Raymond James Stadium	Buccaneers 24 Vikings 17
12-09-99	Nashville	Adelphia Coliseum	Titans 21 Raiders 14
– 85 –			
12-12-99	San Francisco	3Comm Park	49ers 26 Falcons 7
12-19-99	Miami	Pro Player Stadium	Dolphins 12 Chargers 9
12-26-99	San Diego	Qualcomm Stadium	Chargers 23 Raiders 20
01-15-00	Jacksonville	Alltel Stadium	Jaguars 62 Dolphins 7
09-03-00	Oakland	Network Assoc. Coliseum	Raiders 9 Chargers 6
– 90 –			
09-10-00	San Diego	Qualcomm Stadium	Saints 28 Chargers 27
09-17-00	Oakland	Network Assoc. Coliseum	Broncos 33 Raiders 24
09-24-00	San Diego	Qualcomm Stadium	Seahawks 20 Chargers 12
10-01-00	Cincinnati	Paul Brown Stadium	Dolphins 31 Bengals 16
10-02-00	Kansas City	Arrowhead Stadium	Chiefs 24 Seahawks 17
– 95 –			
10-08-00	San Diego	Qualcomm Stadium	Broncos 21 Chargers 7
10-15-00	Chicago	Soldier Field	Vikings 28 Bears 16
10-16-00	Nashville	Adelphia Coliseum	Titans 27 Jaguars 13

DATE	CITY	STADIUM	SCORE
10-19-00	Tampa	Raymond James Stadium	Lions 28 Buccaneers 14
10-22-00	Oakland	Network Assoc. Coliseum	Raiders 31 Seahawks 3
– 100 –			
10-29-00	San Diego	Qualcomm Stadium	Raiders 15 Chargers 13
11-05-00	Oakland	Network Assoc. Coliseum	Raiders 49 Chiefs 31
11-12-00	San Diego	Qualcomm Stadium	Dolphins 17 Chargers 7
11-19-00	East Rutherford	Giants Stadium	Lions 31 Giants 21
11-26-00	San Diego	Qualcomm Stadium	Chargers 17 Chiefs 16
– 105 –			
12-03-00	San Diego	Qualcomm Stadium	49ers 45 Chargers 17
12-10-00	Baltimore	PSINet Stadium	Ravens 24 Chargers 3
12-17-00	San Francisco	3Comm Park	49ers 17 Bears 0
12-24-00	San Diego	Qualcomm Stadium	Steelers 34 Chargers 21
09-09-01	San Diego	Qualcomm Stadium	Chargers 30 Washington 3
– 110 –			
09-23-01	San Francisco	3Comm Park	Rams 30 49ers 26
09-30-01	San Diego	Qualcomm Stadium	Chargers 28 Bengals 14
10-07-01	Cleveland	Cleveland Browns Stadium	Browns 20 Chargers 16
10-14-01	East Rutherford	Giants Stadium	Jets 21 Dolphins 17
10-21-01	San Diego	Qualcomm Stadium	Chargers 27 Broncos 10

DATE	CITY	STADIUM	SCORE
– 115 –			
10-28-01	San Diego	Qualcomm Stadium	Chargers 27 Bills 24
10-29-01	Pittsburgh	Heinz Field	Steelers 34 Titans 7
11-04-01	San Diego	Qualcomm Stadium	Chiefs 25 Chargers 20
11-05-01	Oakland	Network Assoc. Coliseum	Raiders 38 Broncos 28
11-11-01	Denver	Invesco Field at Mile High	Broncos 26 Chargers 16
– 120 –			
11-18-01	Oakland	Network Assoc. Coliseum	Raiders 34 Chargers 24
11-25-01	San Diego	Qualcomm Stadium	Cardinals 20 Chargers 17
12-02-01	Oakland	Network Assoc. Coliseum	Cardinals 34 Raiders 31
12-09-01	Tempe	Sun Devil Stadium	Washington 20 Cardinals 10
12-15-01	San Diego	Qualcomm Stadium	Raiders 13 Chargers 6
– 125 –			
12-16-01	San Francisco	3Comm Park	49ers 21 Dolphins 0
12-22-01	San Francisco	3Comm Park	49ers 13 Eagles 3
12-23-01	Tempe	Sun Devil Stadium	Cardinals 17 Cowboys 10
12-30-01	San Diego	Qualcomm Stadium	Seahawks 25 Chargers 22
01-06-02	Oakland	Network Assoc. Coliseum	Jets 24 Raiders 22
– 130 –			
09-08-02	Green Bay	Lambeau Field	Packers 37 Falcons 34

DATE	CITY	STADIUM	SCORE
09-09-02	Foxboro	Gillette Stadium	Patriots 30 Steelers 14
09-15-02	San Diego	Qualcomm Stadium	Chargers 24 Texans 3
09-22-02	Houston	Reliant Stadium	Colts 23 Texans 3
09-23-02	Tampa	Raymond James Stadium	Buccaneers 26 Rams 14
– 135 –			
09-29-02	San Diego	Qualcomm Stadium	Chargers 21 Patriots 14
09-30-02	Baltimore	Ravens Stadium	Ravens 34 Broncos 23
10-06-02	San Francisco	SF Stad, at Candlestick Point	49ers 37 Rams 13
10-13-02	San Diego	Qualcomm Stadium	Chargers 35 Chiefs 34
10-20-02	Oakland	Network Assoc. Coliseum	Chargers 27 Raiders 21
– 140 –			
10-27-02	Baltimore	Ravens Stadium	Steelers 31 Ravens 18
10-27-02	Landover	FedEx Field	Washington 26 Colts 21
11-03-02	San Diego	Qualcomm Stadium	Jets 44 Chargers 13
11-04-02	Green Bay	Lambeau Field	Packers 24 Dolphins 10
11-10-02	San Francisco	SF Stad. at Candlestick Point	49ers 17 Chiefs 13
– 145 –			
11-17-02	San Diego	Qualcomm Stadium	Chargers 20 49ers 17
11-24-02	Tempe	Sun Devil Stadium	Raiders 41 Cardinals 30
11-25-02	San Francisco	SF Stad. at Candlestick Point	Eagles 38 49ers 17

DATE	CITY	STADIUM	SCORE
12-01-02	San Diego	Qualcomm Stadium	Chargers 30 Broncos 27
12-02-02	Oakland	Network Assoc. Coliseum	Raiders 26 Jets 20
– 150 –			
12-08-02	San Diego	Qualcomm Stadium	Raiders 27 Chargers 7
12-15-02	San Francisco	SF Stad. at Candlestick Point	Packers 20 49ers 14
12-21-02	Tempe	Sun Devil Stadium	49ers 17 Cardinals 14
12-22-02	Oakland	Network Assoc. Coliseum	Raiders 28 Broncos 16
12-29-02	San Diego	Qualcomm Stadium	Seahawks 31 Chargers 28
– 155 –			
01-26-03	San Diego	Qualcomm Stadium	Buccaneers 48 Raiders 21
09-14-03	San Diego	Qualcomm Stadium	Broncos 37 Chargers 13
09-21-03	San Diego	Qualcomm Stadium	Ravens 24 Chargers 10
09-28-03	Oakland	Network Assoc. Coliseum	Raiders 34 Chargers 31
10-05-03	Philadelphia	Lincoln Financial Field	Eagles 27 Washington 25
– 160 –			
10-12-03	Tempe	Sun Devil Stadium	Ravens 26 Cardinals 18
10-19-03	Cleveland	Cleveland Browns Stadium	Chargers 26 Browns 20
10-27-03	Tempe	Sun Devil Stadium	Dolphins 26 Chargers 10
11-02-03	Chicago	Soldier Field	Bears 20 Chargers 7
11-09-03	San Diego	Qualcomm Stadium	Chargers 42 Vikings 28

DATE	CITY	STADIUM	SCORE
– 165 –			
11-16-03	Oakland	Network Assoc. Coliseum	Raiders 28 Vikings 18
11-17-03	San Francisco	SF Stad. at Candlestick Point	49ers 30 Steelers 14
11-23-03	San Diego	Qualcomm Stadium	Bengals 34 Chargers 27
11-30-03	San Diego	Qualcomm Stadium	Chiefs 28 Chargers 24
12-14-03	San Diego	Qualcomm Stadium	Packers 37 Chargers 21
– 170 –			
12-22-03	Oakland	Network Assoc. Coliseum	Packers 41 Raiders 7
12-28-03	San Diego	Qualcomm Stadium	Chargers 21 Raiders 14
09-19-04	San Diego	Qualcomm Stadium	Jets 34 Chargers 28
09-26-04	Oakland	Network Assoc. Coliseum	Raiders 30 Buccaneers 20
10-03-04	San Diego	Qualcomm Stadium	Chargers 38 Titans 17
– 175 –			
10-10-04	San Diego	Qualcomm Stadium	Chargers 34 Jaguars 21
10-24-04	Tempe	Sun Devil Stadium	Cardinals 25 Seahawks 17
10-31-04	San Diego	Qualcomm Stadium	Chargers 42 Raiders 14
11-07-04	San Diego	Qualcomm Stadium	Chargers 43 Saints 17
11-14-04	Tempe	Sun Devil Stadium	Cardinals 17 Giants 14
– 180 –			
11-28-04	Tempe	Sun Devil Stadium	Jets 13 Cardinals 3

DATE	CITY	STADIUM	SCORE
12-05-04	San Diego	Qualcomm Stadium	Chargers 20 Broncos 17
12-12-04	San Diego	Qualcomm Stadium	Chargers 31 Buccaneers 24
12-18-04	San Francisco	Monster Park	Washington 26 49ers 16
12-19-04	Oakland	Network Assoc. Coliseum	Raiders 40 Titans 35
– 185 –			
01-02-05	San Diego	Qualcomm Stadium	Chargers 24 Chiefs 17
01-08-05	San Diego	Qualcomm Stadium	Jets 20 Chargers 17
09-11-05	San Diego	Qualcomm Stadium	Cowboys 28 Chargers 24
09-18-05	Green Bay	Lambeau Field	Browns 26 Packers 24
09-25-05	San Diego	Qualcomm Stadium	Chargers 45 Giants 23
– 190 –			
10-02-05	Oakland	McAfee Coliseum	Raiders 19 Cowboys 13
10-09-05	Tempe	Sun Devil Stadium	Panthers 24 Cardinals 20
10-10-05	San Diego	Qualcomm Stadium	Steelers 24 Chargers 22
10-16-05	Oakland	McAfee Coliseum	Chargers 27 Raiders 14
10-23-05	Cleveland	Cleveland Browns Stadium	Lions 13 Browns 10
– 195 –			
10-30-05	San Diego	Qualcomm Stadium	Chargers 28 Chiefs 20
11-06-05	San Francisco	Monster Park	Giants 26 49ers 16
11-13-05	Pittsburgh	Heinz Field	Steelers 34 Browns 21

DATE	CITY	STADIUM	SCORE
11-14-05	Philadelphia	Lincoln Financial Field	Cowboys 21 Eagles 20
11-20-05	San Diego	Qualcomm Stadium	Chargers 48 Bills 10
– 200 –			
11-27-05	Tempe	Sun Devil Stadium	Jaguars 24 Cardinals 17
12-04-05	Baton Rouge	LSU Tiger Stadium	Buccaneers 10 Saints 3
12-11-05	San Diego	Qualcomm Stadium	Dolphins 23 Chargers 21
12-18-05	Oakland	McAfee Coliseum	Browns 9 Raiders 7
12-24-05	Tempe	Sun Devil Stadium	Cardinals 27 Eagles 21
– 205 –			
12-31-05	San Diego	Qualcomm Stadium	Broncos 23 Chargers 7
01-01-06	San Francisco	Monster Park	49ers 20 Texans 17
09-10-06	Glendale	Cardinals Stadium	Cardinals 34 49ers 27
09-11-06	Oakland	McAfee Coliseum	Chargers 27 Raiders 0
09-17-06	San Diego	Qualcomm Stadium	Chargers 40 Titans 7
– 210 –			
09-24-06	San Francisco	Monster Park	Eagles 38 49ers 24
10-01-06	Kansas City	Arrowhead Stadium	Chiefs 41 49ers 0
10-02-06	Philadelphia	Lincoln Financial Field	Eagles 31 Packers 9
10-08-06	San Diego	Qualcomm Stadium	Chargers 23 Steelers 13
10-15-06	San Francisco	Monster Park	Chargers 48 49ers 19

DATE	CITY	STADIUM	SCORE
\- 215 \-			
10-16-06	Glendale	Univ. of Phoenix Stadium	Bears 24 Cardinals 23
10-22-06	Cleveland	Cleveland Browns Stadium	Broncos 17 Browns 7
10-29-06	San Diego	Qualcomm Stadium	Chargers 38 Rams 24
11-05-06	San Diego	Qualcomm Stadium	Chargers 32 Browns 25
11-12-06	Oakland	McAfee Coliseum	Broncos 17 Raiders 13
\- 220 \-			
11-19-06	Houston	Reliant Stadium	Bills 24 Texans 21
11-26-06	San Diego	Qualcomm Stadium	Chargers 21 Raiders 14
12-03-06	Oakland	McAfee Coliseum	Texans 23 Raiders 14
12-10-06	San Diego	Qualcomm Stadium	Chargers 48 Broncos 20
12-17-06	San Diego	Qualcomm Stadium	Chargers 20 Chiefs 9
\- 225 \-			
12-23-06	Oakland	McAfee Coliseum	Chiefs 20 Raiders 9
12-24-06	San Francisco	Monster Park	Cardinals 26 49ers 20
12-25-06	Miami Gardens	Dolphin Stadium	Jets 13 Dolphins 10
12-31-06	San Diego	Qualcomm Stadium	Chargers 27 Cardinals 20
01-14-07	San Diego	Qualcomm Stadium	Patriots 24 Chargers 21
\- 230 \-			
09-09-07	San Diego	Qualcomm Stadium	Chargers 14 Bears 3

DATE	CITY	STADIUM	SCORE
09-10-07	San Francisco	Monster Park	49ers 20 Cardinals 17
09-16-07	Charlotte	Bank of America Stadium	Texans 34 Panthers 21
09-17-07	Philadelphia	Lincoln Financial Field	Washington 20 Eagles 10
09-23-07	Green Bay	Lambeau Field	Packers 31 Chargers 24
– 235 –			
09-30-07	San Diego	Qualcomm Stadium	Chiefs 30 Chargers 16
10-07-07	San Francisco	Monster Park	Ravens 9 49ers 7
10-14-07	San Diego	Qualcomm Stadium	Chargers 28 Raiders 14
10-21-07	Oakland	McAfee Coliseum	Chiefs 12 Raiders 10
10-28-07	San Diego	Qualcomm Stadium	Chargers 35 Texans 10
– 240 –			
10-29-07	Denver	Invesco Field at Mile High	Packers 19 Broncos 13
11-04-07	Cleveland	Cleveland Browns Stadium	Browns 33 Seahawks 30
11-05-07	Pittsburgh	Heinz Field	Steelers 38 Ravens 7
11-11-07	San Diego	Qualcomm Stadium	Chargers 23 Colts 21
11-18-07	San Francisco	Monster Park	Rams 13 49ers 9
– 245 –			
11-25-07	San Diego	Qualcomm Stadium	Chargers 32 Ravens 14
12-02-07	Glendale	Univ. of Phoenix Stadium	Cardinals 27 Browns 21
12-09-07	San Francisco	Monster Park	Vikings 27 49ers 7

DATE	CITY	STADIUM	SCORE
12-13-07	Houston	Reliant Stadium	Texans 31 Broncos 13
12-15-07	San Francisco	Monster Park	49ers 20 Bengals 13
- 250 -			
12-16-07	San Diego	Qualcomm Stadium	Chargers 51 Lions 14
12-23-07	San Francisco	Monster Park	49ers 21 Buccaneers 19
12-24-07	San Diego	Qualcomm Stadium	Chargers 23 Broncos 3
12-30-07	Glendale	Univ. of Phoenix Stadium	Cardinals 48 Rams 19
01-06-08	San Diego	Qualcomm Stadium	Chargers 17 Titans 6
- 255 -			
02-03-08	Glendale	Univ. of Phoenix Stadium	Giants 17 Patriots 14
09-07-08	San Diego	Qualcomm Stadium	Panthers 26 Chargers 24
09-08-08	Oakland	McAfee Coliseum	Broncos 41 Raiders 14
09-14-08	Glendale	Univ. of Phoenix Stadium	Cardinals 31 Dolphins 10
09-21-08	Philadelphia	Lincoln Financial Field	Eagles 15 Steelers 6
- 260 -			
09-22-08	San Diego	Qualcomm Stadium	Chargers 48 Jets 29
09-28-08	Chicago	Soldier Field	Bears 24 Eagles 20
09-29-08	Pittsburgh	Heinz Field	Steelers 23 Ravens 20
10-05-08	San Francisco	Candlestick Park	Patriots 30 49ers 21
10-12-08	San Diego	Qualcomm Stadium	Chargers 30 Patriots 10

DATE	CITY	STADIUM	SCORE
– 265 –			
10-19-08	Landover	FedEx Field	Washington 14 Browns 11
10-26-08	San Francisco	Candlestick Park	Seahawks 34 49ers 13
11-02-08	Oakland	Oakland-Alameda County Coliseum	Falcons 24 Raiders 0
11-09-08	San Diego	Qualcomm Stadium	Chargers 20 Chiefs 19
11-10-08	Glendale	Univ. of Phoenix Stadium	Cardinals 29 49ers 24
– 270 –			
11-16-08	Pittsburgh	Heinz Field	Steelers 11 Chargers 10
11-23-08	San Diego	Qualcomm Stadium	Colts 23 Chargers 20
11-30-08	San Diego	Qualcomm Stadium	Falcons 22 Chargers 16
12-01-08	Houston	Reliant Stadium	Texans 30 Jaguars 17
12-04-08	San Diego	Qualcomm Stadium	Chargers 34 Raiders 7
– 275 –			
12-07-08	Nashville	LP Field	Titans 28 Browns 9
12-08-08	Charlotte	Bank of America Stadium	Panthers 38 Buccaneers 23
12-14-08	Oakland	Oakland-Alameda County Coliseum	Patriots 49 Raiders 26
12-18-08	Jacksonville	Jacksonville Muni. Stadium	Colts 31 Jaguars 24
12-21-08	Tampa	Raymond James Stadium	Chargers 41 Buccaneers 24
– 280 –			
12-28-08	San Diego	Qualcomm Stadium	Chargers 52 Broncos 21

DATE	CITY	STADIUM	SCORE
01-03-09	San Diego	Qualcomm Stadium	Chargers 23 Colts 17
01-18-09	Glendale	Univ. of Phoenix Stadium	Cardinals 32 Eagles 25
09-13-09	Glendale	Univ. of Phoenix Stadium	49ers 20 Cardinals 16
09-14-09	Oakland	Oakland-Alameda County Coliseum	Chargers 24 Raiders 20
– 285 –			
09-20-09	San Diego	Qualcomm Stadium	Ravens 31 Chargers 26
09-27-09	San Diego	Qualcomm Stadium	Chargers 23 Dolphins 13
10-04-09	Cleveland	Cleveland Browns Stadium	Bengals 23 Browns 20
10-04-09	Pittsburgh	Heinz Field	Steelers 38 Chargers 28
10-11-09	Kansas City	Arrowhead Stadium	Cowboys 26 Chiefs 20
– 290 –			
10-18-09	Oakland	Oakland-Alameda County Coliseum	Raiders 13 Eagles 9
10-19-09	San Diego	Qualcomm Stadium	Broncos 34 Chargers 23
10-25-09	Oakland	Oakland-Alameda County Coliseum	Jets 38 Raiders 0
11-01-09	San Diego	Qualcomm Stadium	Chargers 24 Raiders 16
11-08-09	San Francisco	Candlestick Park	Titans 34 49ers 27
– 295 –			
11-09-09	Denver	Invesco Field at Mile High	Steelers 28 Broncos 10
11-12-09	San Francisco	Candlestick Park	49ers 10 Bears 6
11-15-09	San Diego	Qualcomm Stadium	Chargers 31 Eagles 23

DATE	CITY	STADIUM	SCORE
11-16-09	Cleveland	Cleveland Browns Stadium	Ravens 16 Browns 0
11-19-09	Charlotte	Bank of America Stadium	Dolphins 24 Panthers 17
– 300 –			
11-22-09	Oakland	Oakland-Alameda County Coliseum	Raiders 20 Bengals 17
11-23-09	Houston	Reliant Stadium	Titans 20 Texans 17
11-29-09	San Diego	Qualcomm Stadium	Chargers 43 Chiefs 14
12-06-09	Glendale	Univ. of Phoenix Stadium	Cardinals 30 Vikings 17
12-13-09	Oakland	Oakland-Alameda County Coliseum	Washington 34 Raiders 13
– 305 –			
12-14-09	San Francisco	Candlestick Park	49ers 24 Cardinals 9
12-17-09	Jacksonville	Jacksonville Muni. Stadium	Colts 35 Jaguars 31
12-20-09	San Diego	Qualcomm Stadium	Chargers 27 Bengals 24
12-27-09	San Francisco	Candlestick Park	49ers 20 Lions 6
01-03-10	San Diego	Qualcomm Stadium	Chargers 23 Washington 20
– 310 –			
01-10-10	Glendale	Univ. of Phoenix Stadium	Cardinals 51 Packers 45
01-17-10	San Diego	Qualcomm Stadium	Jets 17 Chargers 14
09-12-10	Chicago	Soldier Field	Bears 19 Lions 14
09-13-10	Kansas City	Arrowhead Stadium	Chiefs 21 Chargers 14
09-19-10	San Diego	Qualcomm Stadium	Chargers 38 Jaguars 13

DATE	CITY	STADIUM	SCORE
— 315 —			
09-20-10	San Francisco	Candlestick Park	Saints 25 49ers 22
09-26-10	Denver	Invesco Field at Mile High	Colts 27 Broncos 13
09-27-10	Chicago	Soldier Field	Bears 20 Packers 17
10-03-10	San Diego	Qualcomm Stadium	Chargers 41 Cardinals 10
10-04-10	Miami Gardens	Sun Life Stadium	Patriots 41 Dolphins 14
— 320 —			
10-10-10	Oakland	Oakland-Alameda County Coliseum	Raiders 35 Chargers 27
10-17-10	San Francisco	Candlestick Park	49ers 17 Raiders 9
10-18-10	Jacksonville	EverBank Field	Titans 30 Jaguars 3
10-24-10	San Diego	Qualcomm Stadium	Patriots 23 Chargers 20
10-31-10	San Diego	Qualcomm Stadium	Chargers 33 Titans 25
— 325 —			
11-07-10	Houston	Reliant Stadium	Chargers 29 Texans 23
11-14-10	Cleveland	Cleveland Browns Stadium	Jets 26 Browns 20
11-14-10	Pittsburgh	Heinz Field	Patriots 39 Steelers 26
11-15-10	Landover	FedEx Field	Eagles 59 Washington 28
11-21-10	San Francisco	Candlestick Park	Buccaneers 21 49ers 0
— 330 —			
11-22-10	San Diego	Qualcomm Stadium	Chargers 35 Broncos 14

DATE	CITY	STADIUM	SCORE
11-28-10	Oakland	Oakland-Alameda County Coliseum	Dolphins 33 Raiders 17
11-29-10	Glendale	Univ. of Phoenix Stadium	49ers 27 Cardinals 6
12-05-10	San Diego	Qualcomm Stadium	Raiders 28 Chargers 13
12-12-10	San Diego	Qualcomm Stadium	Chargers 31 Chiefs 0
– 335 –			
12-13-10	Houston	Reliant Stadium	Ravens 34 Texans 28
12-16-10	San Diego	Qualcomm Stadium	Chargers 34 49ers 7
12-19-10	Oakland	Oakland-Alameda County Coliseum	Raiders 39 Broncos 23
12-26-10	Oakland	Oakland-Alameda County Coliseum	Colts 31 Raiders 26
01-02-11	San Francisco	Candlestick Park	49ers 38 Cardinals 7
– 340 –			
09-11-11	San Diego	Qualcomm Stadium	Chargers 24 Vikings 17
09-18-11	San Francisco	Candlestick Park	Cowboys 27 49ers 24
09-25-11	San Diego	Qualcomm Stadium	Chargers 20 Chiefs 17
10-02-11	San Diego	Qualcomm Stadium	Chargers 26 Dolphins 16
10-09-11	San Francisco	Candlestick Park	49ers 48 Buccaneers 3
– 345 –			
10-16-11	Oakland	O.co Coliseum	Raiders 24 Browns 17
10-23-11	Glendale	Univ. of Phoenix Stadium	Steelers 32 Cardinals 20
10-30-11	San Francisco	Candlestick Park	49ers 20 Browns 10

DATE	CITY	STADIUM	SCORE
11-06-11	San Diego	Qualcomm Stadium	Packers 45 Chargers 38
11-10-11	San Diego	Qualcomm Stadium	Raiders 24 Chargers 17
– 350 –			
11-13-11	Cleveland	Cleveland Browns Stadium	Rams 13 Browns 12
11-17-11	Denver	Sports Auth. Field at Mile High	Broncos 17 Jets 13
11-20-11	Chicago	Soldier Field	Bears 31 Chargers 20
11-27-11	San Diego	Qualcomm Stadium	Broncos 16 Chargers 13
12-04-11	Tampa	Raymond James Stadium	Panthers 38 Buccaneers 19
– 355 –			
12-05-11	Jacksonville	EverBank Field	Chargers 38 Jaguars 14
12-11-11	San Diego	Qualcomm Stadium	Chargers 37 Bills 10
12-18-11	San Diego	Qualcomm Stadium	Chargers 34 Ravens 14
12-19-11	San Francisco	Candlestick Park	49ers 20 Steelers 3
01-01-12	Oakland	O.co Coliseum	Chargers 38 Raiders 26
– 360 –			
01-07-12	Houston	Reliant Stadium	Texans 31 Bengals 10
01-14-12	San Francisco	Candlestick Park	49ers 36 Saints 32
01-22-12	San Francisco	Candlestick Park	Giants 20 49ers 17
09-09-12	Glendale	Univ. of Phoenix Stadium	Cardinals 20 Seahawks 16
09-10-12	Oakland	O.co Coliseum	Chargers 22 Raiders 14

DATE	CITY	STADIUM	SCORE
- 365 -			
09-16-12	San Diego	Qualcomm Stadium	Chargers 38 Titans 10
09-20-12	Charlotte	Bank of America Stadium	Giants 36 Panthers 7
09-23-12	San Diego	Qualcomm Stadium	Falcons 27 Chargers 3
09-30-12	Denver	Sports Auth. Field at Mile High	Broncos 37 Raiders 6
10-07-12	San Francisco	Candlestick Park	49ers 45 Bills 3
- 370 -			
10-11-12	Nashville	LP Field	Titans 26 Steelers 23
10-14-12	Glendale	Univ. of Phoenix Stadium	Bills 19 Cardinals 16
10-15-12	San Diego	Qualcomm Stadium	Broncos 35 Chargers 24
10-18-12	San Francisco	Candlestick Park	49ers 13 Seahawks 3
10-21-12	Oakland	O.co Coliseum	Raiders 26 Jaguars 23
- 375 -			
10-28-12	Cleveland	Cleveland Browns Stadium	Browns 7 Chargers 6
10-29-12	Glendale	Univ. of Phoenix Stadium	49ers 24 Cardinals 3
11-01-12	San Diego	Qualcomm Stadium	Chargers 31 Chiefs 13
11-04-12	Landover	FedEx Field	Panthers 21 Washington 13
11-11-12	Tampa	Raymond James Stadium	Buccaneers 34 Chargers 24
- 380 -			
11-18-12	Oakland	O.co Coliseum	Saints 38 Raiders 17

DATE	CITY	STADIUM	SCORE
11-19-12	San Francisco	Candlestick Park	49ers 32 Bears 7
11-25-12	San Diego	Qualcomm Stadium	Ravens 16 Chargers 13
12-02-12	San Diego	Qualcomm Stadium	Bengals 20 Chargers 13
12-06-12	Oakland	O.co Coliseum	Broncos 26 Raiders 13
– 385 –			
12-09-12	San Francisco	Candlestick Park	49ers 27 Dolphins 13
12-16-12	San Diego	Qualcomm Stadium	Panthers 31 Chargers 7
12-23-12	Glendale	Univ. of Phoenix Stadium	Bears 28 Cardinals 13
12-30-12	San Diego	Qualcomm Stadium	Chargers 24 Raiders 21
01-12-13	San Francisco	Candlestick Park	49ers 45 Packers 31
– 390 –			
09-08-13	San Francisco	Candlestick Park	49ers 34 Packers 28
09-09-13	San Diego	Qualcomm Stadium	Texans 31 Chargers 28
09-15-13	Philadelphia	Lincoln Financial Field	Chargers 33 Eagles 30
09-22-13	Nashville	LP Field	Titans 20 Chargers 17
09-29-13	San Diego	Qualcomm Stadium	Chargers 30 Cowboys 21
– 395 –			
10-03-13	Cleveland	FirstEnergy Stadium	Browns 37 Bills 24
10-06-13	San Francisco	Candlestick Park	49ers 34 Texans 3
10-13-13	San Francisco	Candlestick Park	49ers 32 Cardinals 20

DATE	CITY	STADIUM	SCORE
10-14-13	San Diego	Qualcomm Stadium	Chargers 19 Colts 9
10-17-13	Glendale	Univ. of Phoenix Stadium	Seahawks 34 Cardinals 22
– 400 –			
10-27-13	Oakland	O.co Coliseum	Raiders 21 Steelers 18
11-03-13	Oakland	O.co Coliseum	Eagles 49 Raiders 20
11-10-13	San Diego	Qualcomm Stadium	Broncos 28 Chargers 20
11-17-13	Denver	Sports Auth. Field at Mile High	Broncos 27 Chiefs 17
11-24-13	Glendale	Univ. of Phoenix Stadium	Cardinals 40 Colts 11
– 405 –			
12-01-13	San Diego	Qualcomm Stadium	Bengals 17 Chargers 10
12-08-13	San Diego	Qualcomm Stadium	Chargers 37 Giants 14
12-15-13	Oakland	O.co Coliseum	Chiefs 56 Raiders 31
12-22-13	San Diego	Qualcomm Stadium	Chargers 26 Raiders 13
12-23-13	San Francisco	Candlestick Park	49ers 34 Falcons 24
– 410 –			
12-29-13	San Diego	Qualcomm Stadium	Chargers 27 Chiefs 24
09-07-14	Chicago	Soldier Field	Bills 23 Bears 20
09-08-14	Glendale	Univ. of Phoenix Stadium	Cardinals 18 Chargers 17
09-14-14	San Diego	Qualcomm Stadium	Chargers 30 Seahawks 21
09-21-14	Glendale	Univ. of Phoenix Stadium	Cardinals 23 49ers 14

DATE	CITY	STADIUM	SCORE
– 415 –			
09-28-14	San Diego	Qualcomm Stadium	Chargers 33 Jaguars 14
09-29-14	Kansas City	Arrowhead Stadium	Chiefs 41 Patriots 14
10-02-14	Green Bay	Lambeau Field	Packers 42 Vikings 10
10-05-14	San Diego	Qualcomm Stadium	Chargers 31 Jets 0
10-09-14	Houston	NRG Stadium	Colts 33 Texans 28
– 420 –			
10-12-14	Cleveland	FirstEnergy Stadium	Browns 31 Steelers 10
10-19-14	San Diego	Qualcomm Stadium	Chiefs 23 Chargers 20
10-23-14	Denver	Sports Auth. Field at Mile High	Broncos 35 Chargers 21
10-26-14	Kansas City	Arrowhead Stadium	Chiefs 34 Rams 7
11-02-14	Santa Clara	Levi's Stadium	Rams 13 49ers 10
– 425 –			
11-09-14	Glendale	Univ. of Phoenix Stadium	Cardinals 31 Rams 14
11-16-14	San Diego	Qualcomm Stadium	Chargers 13 Raiders 6
11-20-14	Oakland	O.co Coliseum	Raiders 24 Chiefs 20
11-23-14	San Diego	Qualcomm Stadium	Chargers 27 Rams 24
11-27-14	Santa Clara	Levi's Stadium	Seahawks 19 49ers 3
– 430 –			
11-30-14	Kansas City	Arrowhead Stadium	Broncos 29 Chiefs 16

DATE	CITY	STADIUM	SCORE
12-04-14	Chicago	Soldier Field	Cowboys 41 Bears 28
12-07-14	Oakland	O.co Coliseum	Raiders 24 49ers 13
12-14-14	Kansas City	Arrowhead Stadium	Chiefs 31 Raiders 13
12-15-14	Chicago	Soldier Field	Saints 31 Bears 15
– 435 –			
12-20-14	Santa Clara	Levi's Stadium	Chargers 38 49ers 35
12-21-14	Oakland	O.co Coliseum	Raiders 26 Bills 24
12-28-14	Santa Clara	Levi's Stadium	49ers 20 Cardinals 17
02-01-15	Glendale	Univ. of Phoenix Stadium	Patriots 28 Seahawks 24
09-13-15	San Diego	Qualcomm Stadium	Chargers 33 Lions 28
– 440 –			
09-14-15	Santa Clara	Levi's Stadium	49ers 20 Vikings 3
09-20-15	Oakland	O.co Coliseum	Raiders 37 Ravens 33
09-27-15	Cleveland	FirstEnergy Stadium	Raiders 27 Browns 20
09-28-15	Green Bay	Lambeau Field	Packers 38 Chiefs 28
10-04-15	San Diego	Qualcomm Stadium	Chargers 30 Browns 27
– 445 –			
10-11-15	Oakland	O.co Coliseum	Broncos 16 Raiders 10
10-12-15	San Diego	Qualcomm Stadium	Steelers 24 Chargers 20
10-25-15	San Diego	Qualcomm Stadium	Raiders 37 Chargers 29

DATE	CITY	STADIUM	SCORE
10-26-15	Glendale	Univ. of Phoenix Stadium	Cardinals 26 Ravens 18
11-01-15	Oakland	O.co Coliseum	Raiders 34 Jets 20
– 450 –			
11-08-15	Santa Clara	Levi's Stadium	49ers 17 Falcons 16
11-09-15	San Diego	Qualcomm Stadium	Bears 22 Chargers 19
11-15-15	Landover	FedEx Field	Washington 47 Saints 14
11-22-15	San Diego	Qualcomm Stadium	Chiefs 33 Chargers 3
12-06-15	San Diego	Qualcomm Stadium	Broncos 17 Chargers 3
– 455 –			
12-10-15	Glendale	Univ. of Phoenix Stadium	Cardinals 23 Vikings 20
12-13-15	Tampa	Raymond James Stadium	Saints 24 Buccaneers 17
12-20-15	San Diego	Qualcomm Stadium	Chargers 30 Dolphins 14
12-24-15	Oakland	O.co Coliseum	Raiders 23 Chargers 20
12-27-15	Glendale	Univ. of Phoenix Stadium	Cardinals 38 Packers 8
– 460 –			
01-03-16	Glendale	Univ. of Phoenix Stadium	Seahawks 36 Cardinals 6
01-16-16	Glendale	Univ. of Phoenix Stadium	Cardinals 26 Packers 20
09-11-16	Glendale	Univ. of Phoenix Stadium	Patriots 23 Cardinals 21
09-18-16	San Diego	Qualcomm Stadium	Chargers 38 Jaguars 14
10-02-16	San Diego	Qualcomm Stadium	Saints 35 Chargers 34

DATE	CITY	STADIUM	SCORE
– 465 –			
10-06-16	Santa Clara	Levi's Stadium	Cardinals 33 49ers 21
10-09-16	Denver	Sports Auth. Field at Mile High	Falcons 23 Broncos 16
10-13-16	San Diego	Qualcomm Stadium	Chargers 21 Broncos 13
10-16-16	Oakland	Oakland-Alameda County Coliseum	Chiefs 26 Raiders 10
10-17-16	Glendale	Univ. of Phoenix Stadium	Cardinals 28 Jets 6
– 470 –			
10-23-16	Philadelphia	Lincoln Financial Field	Eagles 21 Vikings 10
10-30-16	Tampa	Raymond James Stadium	Raiders 30 Buccaneers 24
11-03-16	Tampa	Raymond James Stadium	Falcons 43 Buccaneers 28
11-06-16	Cleveland	FirstEnergy Stadium	Cowboys 35 Browns 10
11-10-16	Baltimore	M&T Bank Stadium	Ravens 28 Browns 7
– 475 –			
11-13-16	San Diego	Qualcomm Stadium	Dolphins 31 Chargers 24
11-20-16	Los Angeles	L.A. Memorial Coliseum	Dolphins 14 Rams 10
11-27-16	Oakland	Oakland-Alameda County Coliseum	Raiders 35 Panthers 32
12-04-16	San Diego	Qualcomm Stadium	Buccaneers 28 Chargers 21
12-11-16	Charlotte	Bank of America Stadium	Panthers 28 Chargers 16
– 480 –			
12-18-16	San Diego	Qualcomm Stadium	Raiders 19 Chargers 16

DATE	CITY	STADIUM	SCORE
12-24-16	Los Angeles	L.A. Memorial Coliseum	49ers 22 Rams 21
01-01-17	San Diego	Qualcomm Stadium	Chiefs 37 Chargers 27
09-10-17	Los Angeles	L.A. Memorial Coliseum	Rams 46 Colts 9
09-17-17	Carson	StubHub Center	Dolphins 19 Chargers 17
– 485 –			
09-21-17	Santa Clara	Levi's Stadium	Rams 41 49ers 39
09-24-17	Carson	StubHub Center	Chiefs 24 Chargers 10
09-25-17	Glendale	Univ. of Phoenix Stadium	Cowboys 28 Cardinals 17
10-01-17	Cleveland	FirstEnergy Stadium	Bengals 31 Browns 7
10-02-17	Kansas City	Arrowhead Stadium	Chiefs 29 Washington 20
– 490 –			
10-08-17	Cleveland	FirstEnergy Stadium	Jets 17 Browns 14
10-09-17	Chicago	Soldier Field	Vikings 20 Bears 17
10-15-17	Baltimore	M&T Bank Stadium	Bears 27 Ravens 24
10-16-17	Nashville	Nissan Stadium	Titans 36 Colts 22
10-19-17	Oakland	Oakland-Alameda County Coliseum	Raiders 31 Chiefs 30
– 495 –			
10-22-17	Pittsburgh	Heinz Field	Steelers 29 Bengals 14
10-23-17	Philadelphia	Lincoln Financial Field	Eagles 34 Washington 24
10-29-17	Landover	FedEx Field	Cowboys 33 Washington 19

DATE	CITY	STADIUM	SCORE
10-30-17	Kansas City	Arrowhead Stadium	Chiefs 29 Broncos 19
11-06-17	Green Bay	Lambeau Field	Lions 30 Packers 17
– 500! –			
11-12-17	Santa Clara	Levi's Stadium	49ers 31 Giants 21
11-19-17	Carson	StubHub Center	Chargers 54 Bills 24
11-26-17	Kansas City	Arrowhead Stadium	Bills 16 Chiefs 10
12-03-17	Carson	StubHub Center	Chargers 19 Browns 10
12-10-17	Carson	StubHub Center	Chargers 30 Washington 13
– 505 –			
12-17-17	Oakland	Oakland-Alameda County Coliseum	Cowboys 20 Raiders 17
12-24-17	Glendale	Univ. of Phoenix Stadium	Cardinals 23 Giants 0
12-31-17	Carson	StubHub Center	Chargers 30 Raiders 10
01-06-18	Los Angeles	L.A. Memorial Coliseum	Falcons 26 Rams 13
09-10-18	Oakland	Oakland-Alameda County Coliseum	Rams 33 Raiders 13
– 510 –			
09-16-18	Los Angeles	L.A. Memorial Coliseum	Rams 34 Cardinals 0
09-23-18	Los Angeles	L.A. Memorial Coliseum	Rams 35 Chargers 23
09-27-18	Los Angeles	L.A. Memorial Coliseum	Rams 38 Vikings 31
09-30-18	Oakland	Oakland-Alameda County Coliseum	Raiders 45 Browns 42
10-18-18	Glendale	State Farm Stadium	Broncos 45 Cardinals 10

DATE	CITY	STADIUM	SCORE
\- 515 \-			
10-28-18	Los Angeles	L.A. Memorial Coliseum	Rams 29 Packers 27
11-01-18	Santa Clara	Levi's Stadium	49ers 34 Raiders 3
11-04-18	Cleveland	FirstEnergy Stadium	Chiefs 37 Browns 21
11-11-18	Los Angeles	L.A. Memorial Coliseum	Rams 36 Seahawks 31
11-18-18	Glendale	State Farm Stadium	Raiders 23 Cardinals 21
\- 520 \-			
11-19-18	Los Angeles	L.A. Memorial Coliseum	Rams 54 Chiefs 51
12-09-18	Santa Clara	Levi's Stadium	49ers 20 Broncos 14
12-16-18	Los Angeles	L.A. Memorial Coliseum	Eagles 30 Rams 23
12-30-18	Los Angeles	L.A. Memorial Coliseum	Rams 48 49ers 32
01-12-19	Los Angeles	L.A. Memorial Coliseum	Rams 30 Cowboys 22
\- 525 \-			
09-08-19	Glendale	State Farm Stadium	Lions 27 Cardinals 27
09-09-19	Oakland	Oakland-Alameda County Coliseum	Raiders 24 Broncos 16
09-29-19	Los Angeles	L.A. Memorial Coliseum	Buccaneers 55 Rams 40
10-06-19	Philadelphia	Lincoln Financial Field	Eagles 31 Jets 6
10-13-19	Glendale	State Farm Stadium	Cardinals 34 Falcons 33
\- 530 \-			
10-27-19	Santa Clara	Levi's Stadium	49ers 51 Panthers 13

DATE	CITY	STADIUM	SCORE
11-03-19	Oakland	Oakland-Alameda County Coliseum	Raiders 31 Lions 24
11-17-19	Los Angeles	L.A. Memorial Coliseum	Rams 17 Bears 7
11-24-19	Santa Clara	Levi's Stadium	49ers 37 Packers 8
11-25-19	Los Angeles	L.A. Memorial Coliseum	Ravens 45 Rams 6
– 535 –			
12-08-19	Los Angeles	L.A. Memorial Coliseum	Rams 28 Seahawks 12
12-15-19	Oakland	Oakland-Alameda County Coliseum	Jaguars 20 Raiders 16
12-22-19	Denver	Empower Field at Mile High	Broncos 27 Lions 17
12-29-19	Los Angeles	L.A. Memorial Coliseum	Rams 31 Cardinals 24
01-11-20	Santa Clara	Levi's Stadium	49ers 27 Vikings 10
– 540 –			
01-19-20	Santa Clara	Levi's Stadium	49ers 37 Packers 20
09-13-21	Las Vegas	Allegiant Stadium	Raiders 33 Ravens 27
09-19-21	Glendale	State Farm Stadium	Cardinals 34 Vikings 33
09-26-21	Cleveland	FirstEnergy Stadium	Browns 26 Bears 6
10-03-21	Santa Clara	Levi's Stadium	Seahawks 28 49ers 21
– 545 –			
10-10-21	Las Vegas	Allegiant Stadium	Bears 20 Raiders 9
10-17-21	Pittsburgh	Heinz Field	Steelers 23 Seahawks 20
10-24-21	Glendale	State Farm Stadium	Cardinals 31 Texans 5

DATE	CITY	STADIUM	SCORE
10-28-21	Glendale	State Farm Stadium	Packers 24 Cardinals 21
10-31-21	Denver	Empower Field at Mile High	Broncos 17 Washington 10
– 550 –